# Manna from Heaven

## And Other True Stories

To John,
With My Best Wishes for a
Happy, Healthy and Prosperous
New Year of 2022.
Christopher Spencer.

## CHRISTOPHER SPENCER

# About the Author

Christopher Spencer (not his real name) has worked in the banking and construction sectors and as an Adviser to Government. He has 50 years of experience in international business and finance and has qualifications in economics, accountancy and banking. He is still active in business and now works on promoting new technologies.

Christopher lives in London with his wife and has two grown-up children. He also has several grandchildren. He likes solitary walks and reading about international politics and world history. But he also reads modern poetry and detective stories.

To my children, with love.

# Contents

# Preface

I have written these stories because they are substantially true and I want to share them with others. They arise from my 50 years of experience in the world of international business and finance. Where I have thought necessary, I have altered the names of my characters, but they are real people who may recognise themselves. If they do and they are troubled by this, then I can only apologise to them. In some cases, I have changed the facts to protect them. I have not changed the names of places or the circumstances. In one case, I have not identified the country involved because the Head of State, whom I met several times, is no longer in charge, but is now being tried for corruption.

Although I retired for a couple of years, I am now back working again, and I find that this work keeps my mind active and supple. I separate out this work, where people know me by my real name, from my humble attempts at story-telling. That is why I use the nom de plume of Christopher Spencer. Somehow, I seem to have produced an unusual "genre"; a series of autobiographical episodes rather than an autobiography. They represent different periods of my life and, within each episode, I may move from the present to the past and even to the future. But that is the nature of my story-telling, and I am hampered by the fact that my stories are all true. I have also used the novelette format, longer than a short story, but not as long as a novella or a novel. I did this because it seemed to suit both my writing style and my content.

I admit that I have taken certain literary licence with the sequence of events to, I hope, provide a more interesting story for my readers. These days, we in the West seem to live in a largely cosy world which, increasingly, is divorced from reality. My belief is that modern technology can often hinder real progress and decision-making; in the end, I believe in people and in their ability to interact and work together for a common aim. Technology can divide people, rather than allowing them to sort out their real problems face-to-face. In many parts of the world, progress based on the standard of living for ordinary people has been very slow and, in some tragic cases, any progress has been destroyed by civil war and continuing social collapse and terrorism. We now face the tragic and debilitating events of a global pandemic. I believe that the effects of this and the resulting rapid development of technology will bring many major changes in society on an international scale. Many of these will be for the good, but we must strongly guard against the possibility that these changes could also prove detrimental to the indomitable human spirit!

My main character, Edwards, is myself. He shows certain aspects of my character and disposition. He is lazy and likes the comforts of life. He likes high living, when he can get it. He is sociable, but hates crowds. But he is capable of hard work, especially with other people, when needed. He has an ability to fit in, especially with foreigners. He can quickly understand a situation, but he is also, at times, a day-dreamer and is always nostalgic. The past always seems somehow more attractive to him, compared with the present.

In my first story, "Manna from Heaven," we meet Edwards, who is considered to be a "high flyer" within the international construction company that employs him. He is paid well, but his work is hard and stressful. Nevertheless, he tries to enjoy the high-life when he can. Then he is sent by his employers on a pilgrimage to find some "Manna from Heaven." Is there really a "Crock of Gold at the end of the Rainbow?" During his journey, both in England and overseas, events and places evoke memories from his childhood and from more recent times.

This story is set in the early 1980's, and it actually happened to me. First, Edwards is sent by train to the West Country to confront an unpleasant individual. Then he is sent to Switzerland to meet a mysterious couple. Finally, in Paris, he meets the head of a powerful American organisation that promises the "Crock of Gold." At the end of his pilgrimage, back in London, he faces a major dilemma. It is so serious that it could threaten his whole future career. Only the secret world of the international intelligence community can really help him, to finally resolve his problem.

In the second autobiographical episode called "The Banker," we meet a younger Edwards, working in the City of London, for a leading stockbroking firm. This story is set in the 1970's, and Edwards has now specialised in the International Bond Market. He is given, as his marketing area, into which he must sell bonds, Italy and the Italian-speaking part of Switzerland. He enjoys this new world of international travel. But, in Milan, he meets a man who is at the centre of the "Dark Heart" of Italian finance and corruption. Edwards is then sent to meet a banker in a small town on the border between Italy and Switzerland. From that meeting, substantial business will flow for Edwards's employers.

But all is not what it seems. Soon doubts begin to grow in Edwards's mind. Then arrests are made and the façade begins to crumble. Along the way, others begin to lose their reputations and their positions. Disgrace, long prison sentences or, in some cases, even violent death, now await some of the participants. Eventually, disillusioned, Edwards leaves the City of London and joins the real world of the international construction business.

"Whispers" is set in the second half of the 1980's and is, again, true. A few words, whispered within the walls of a great fortress, could be of vital importance. But nobody, who needs to know their real meaning, can understand them. They need to be correctly interpreted so that top-level decisions can be made. Edwards is already steeped in the "Enigma of Mirrors" that is the Cold War. Even at university, he has seen radicalisation take place, and since then, others have used him to hide their true intent. He is then asked to help again; this time, he must persuade his wife to carry out a vital task.

With her expert help, the true meaning of the whispered words becomes clear. Decisions are made at the very top of the British Government, and the course of world history is changed.

The fourth true story is set mainly in Turkey in the mid-1980's and concerns a major new construction project, "The Byzantine Bridge," which Edwards is asked to help finance. Everything, including the usual intrigue he has to face, seems to go well. But then, Edwards is sent on what he calls a "Mission Impossible," to rescue the project for his employers. He insists on taking a colleague; a man who is a true "survivor" and is highly experienced in working in difficult conditions, in countries located behind the "Iron Curtain."

In Ankara, they work under close Turkish surveillance, to try and achieve success but, at every turn, difficulties seem to arise. Edwards is given full diplomatic support and, eventually, has to decide that only a "top-level" message might save the day. He is asked to write this himself, and then it is conveyed to the right people within the Turkish Government. But others are at work, with bribery and deception, to undermine his efforts and win the project for themselves.

The fifth story, called "On the Road," is set mainly in South East Asia in the late 1980's. Again, Edwards is given what he terms a "Mission Impossible," to find finance for an essential motorway project which, all the experts say, cannot be found. He is working at the top level within Indonesia, as well as in both London and Washington. It is exhausting work, with constant international travel. Slowly, he begins to see a possible solution and starts to get the pieces of this complex jigsaw puzzle into place. If he can achieve it, it will bring benefit for his own company, for Britain and for Indonesia, and change the way that finance can be done.

However, within his own company, there are those who do not seem to want him to succeed. People often have their own "agendas," and this seems to apply to an unpleasant, senior man, to whom Edwards has to report. His actions are not supportive of Edwards, and, eventually, he frustrates Edwards's carefully laid plans. His reason may be his own selfish interests. This results in the loss of the project for Edwards's employers and for Britain but, fortunately, not the loss of some of Edwards's hard work and ideas.

In the sixth autobiographical episode, "Tradecraft," set in the late 1990's, Edwards is in Africa. Because of his long experience of the international world, he is now employed to help promote British exports. But it is a difficult and sometimes dangerous task. He often has to balance his sense of morality, against what is necessary in order to get business. He is working with a man, from an unnamed African country, who should have all the right connections. Through him, he should be able to get to the very top of government. But what goes on in this country is very difficult to understand and he has to seek some advice. This is delivered to him, but under conditions of great secrecy.

When he has time on his hands, he compares his experiences here with another African country that he has visited. He is then asked to set up a personal program for a top-level African politician to visit London. Soon after this visit, the situation begins to unravel. Dismissals and arrests occur and recriminations begin to fly.

The final true story is called "Tremors" and is set in the mid-1990's. Edwards is now part of a government-funded organisation, set up to help British exporters. One of his colleagues works closely with the intelligence services. One day, a long-standing friend of Edwards, introduces him to a journalist for a secret meeting. What this man has to say is hair-raising. At the end of their discussions, this man makes an astonishing offer. Edwards now has the responsibility to convey this offer to those in government who may be able to take the necessary action.

Using his colleague, he tries to do this. But they are both met with obfuscation and finally a refusal to act. Along the way, Edwards muses about the naivety of his long-standing friend, who had introduced him to this man. Edwards can now do no more with the offer that has been made. But the refusal to take up the offer, made by the journalist, seems to lead finally to unforeseen and horrific consequences.

Some of these stories may raise controversy. I hope that they may educate some of my readers about aspects of the international world that they do not know or, may even, not want to know. They may also introduce a different perspective on some of the events in the world of the late 20$^{th}$ and early 21$^{st}$ centuries. The truth can often be very inconvenient, and I will, no doubt, be criticised. I am now of advanced years, but I find that often my recollection of these few events in my past life, is clearer than events that have happened to me just a few months ago. I am therefore endeavouring to get these earlier events down on paper before I forget them, or before my inevitable demise.

I was born in the early 1940's and have therefore seen many changes. As far as the current world is concerned, modern technology certainly has its advantages. But it is becoming increasingly clear that it also has many disadvantages. Virtual Reality is definitely not Reality, and sitting staring at a screen for hours is unhealthy. Only recently, we have seen the effects of major international hacking using ransomware with criminal intent. But, like gunpowder and the atomic bomb, this technology cannot be un-invented. It brings with it, I believe, misunderstandings, unreality, unemployment, crime, terrorism, pornography and obesity. It also brings, I believe, increasing business inefficiencies.

A wise man, for whom I once worked, one day told me about the "factor of two point seven." This meant, that when you were planning a major project, you should realise that it would eventually cost 2.7 times more than you first estimated and it would take 2.7 times longer to complete it, than you had anticipated. I fear that we may now be approaching a "factor of five point four!" Too many emails, to too many people, and waiting for them all to give their consent, which they will never do. This is because there are just too many emails to reply to. There is also, too often, an attempted, ignorant micro-management from the centre when, in fact, those who are "at the coal-face" or "out in the field," really know best what is happening and what to do. It is their views and their personal judgement that should be followed.

Brave people have to make big decisions, on their own, because often only they know the complete facts. Otherwise, the world will drift towards entropy. Often, a personal judgement must be made quickly and a personal responsibility must be taken. As I confront the modern world, I cannot but recall just two of the lines, written in 1934 by T. S. Elliot, from his poem "Choruses From The Rock." I think that they provide a warning to us all.

*"Where is the wisdom we have lost in knowledge?*
*Where is the knowledge we have lost in information?"*

**— Christopher Spencer**
London. December, 2020.

# Manna From Heaven

-

This story and the following stories are substantially true. Names but not places have been changed. Certain literary licence has been taken with the sequence of events.

-

*"There's no discouragement,*
*Shall make him once relent,*
*His first avowed intent,*
*To be a pilgrim."*


*"He Who Would Valiant Be."*
**— Hymn by John Bunyan.**

# 1

"You realise that we are in mortal danger!"

Edwards looked at the man, across the desk, who had just said these words. He had his jacket off, had gone to fat and there were signs of sweat under his armpits. He was watching Edwards carefully, to see the effect of what he had just said. Edwards sat straight upright in his hard chair, on the other side of the cheap desk. He had not removed his jacket and tie, even though it was very warm in the stuffy, front room of the small, terraced house.

Edwards looked out of the window. It was late May, in England, in 1982. They were on the ground floor of a house on the Green. Across the well-manicured grass, the great Gothic front of the cathedral glistened in the sunshine; it had stood there for over 600 years. Edwards had once visited it when he was much younger and had been staying with his parents at a nearby coastal resort. He knew that it had the longest uninterrupted vaulted ceiling in England. He well remembered that ancient vault; he turned back to the man he had just met. "Are we?" he asked quietly, and he did not bother to hide the disbelief in his voice.

Yesterday had been rather an unfortunate day. He had got into his office late. The traffic into the West London suburb where the "Red Edifice", as he called the tall office building, stood had been much worse than usual. Already there were calls waiting to be returned. Liz, his Personal Assistant, fussed around.

"Mr. Jones from Marketing wants to see you," she said. He knew Jones, and he did not want to be excited by his enthusiasm so early in the day.

"Just get me a coffee, please, Liz" he pleaded. "I've had an awful drive in this morning!"

His thick windows failed to muffle properly the sound of the heavy traffic on the flyover outside; to the east lay the centre of the city and to the west Heathrow Airport. Both had now become the joint centres of his world since he had moved to London some fifteen years before.

He drove in to work because his employers gave him a car and free petrol. He was only taxed on part of the cost, so there was no contest between that and an expensive season ticket and standing and sweating with the other commuters on what were, inevitably, late or non-existent trains. He did not like crowds; he had never done so. The thought of going to some major sporting event appalled him. He even preferred solitary walks rather than having someone with him that he then had to talk to. Having said that, he was thought to be very sociable in the office, and people always wanted to see him and ask his opinion.

He was considered a "high flyer," having been recruited from the City of London, where he had worked for several top merchant banks and a stockbroker. This was where he had gained his first real taste of the international world. Now he had to deal with the world-wide business of a large group of construction and engineering companies. He had always been old beyond his years, but the current job tested him beyond all reasonable levels. He was expected to give authoritative advice to directors, lawyers and other staff on all matters financial. When he got home at night, exhausted from the day and another long drive, all he wanted to do was to eat and sit down in front of the television. He did not understand how his wife put up with him!

Opposite him on his office wall was his "Worry Picture"; a small reproduction of one of Monet's pictures of water lilies in his garden at Giverny. Whenever Edwards was stressed, usually on the telephone, he would look long into the colours and the calm water. Liz brought him in a steaming mug of white coffee with two spoons of sugar; this would be the first of several he would need that morning, just to keep going. He always said that "If he had not dealt with the affairs of six different countries by the time of his second mug, it was a quiet morning."

He did not get to Jones's office until three in the afternoon. "Come in, come in," beamed the fussy little man, and he conducted Edwards to a comfortable chair in front of the desk. "It's a great opportunity!" exclaimed Jones. "They are offering us long-term loans at cheap interest rates."

"Who are?" Edwards asked.

"They are based in Washington," continued Jones, ignoring the question. He produced two sheets of paper and handed them to Edwards.

"Can I keep these?" asked Edwards, who could not read and listen to Jones at the same time. Jones pressed on with some increasingly confusing points; Edwards asked what he thought were some pertinent questions, then left.

Back in his office, he read the two sheets of paper carefully. It was as Jones had said. An organisation in the American federal capital city of Washington D.C. was willing to lend almost unlimited sums of money in US dollars to projects on an international basis. All they required was a guarantee from an acceptable government, and they were willing to lend for up to 20 years at fixed, low interest rates. For an international contractor, this was "Manna from Heaven!" His group of companies could win major contracts by linking their construction skills with this attractive funding.

 Against his better judgement, Edwards had been persuaded to take the train the following day down to a West Country city. Jones had given him a name and an address. He knew that the day after, the work would be piled up on his desk and there would probably be dozens of telephone calls to return. But a break away from the office was welcome. He had not been on an overseas trip for some time; compared with the pressure of work back in the office, he almost viewed these trips now as holidays! "As long as it is on your budget," he had muttered to Jones, as he had put the telephone down, after he had called Jones to tell him that he was prepared to investigate this matter further.

# 2

The fat man droned on in his unmistakable West Country accent. He had handed some papers to Edwards. Again, Edwards could not read them and listen to what the man had to say. He had presented his business card to the man in order to get something definite returned, but nothing like that had been given to him. His mind drifted back to his early start that morning; a series of Tube trains to Paddington Station and then the comfortable first class seat on the Inter- City Express. Whenever he travelled, Edwards wanted to eat; his philosophy was that when on the move, you should eat when you could, as you never knew when the next meal would be available. He made his way, down the swaying train corridor, to the dining car. It was all on the Marketing budget anyway!

"A full English Breakfast, sir?" asked the white-coated attendant.

Edwards nodded. "And coffee, please," he said. His first tea and coffee of the day at his home now seemed a long time ago.

Edwards looked out of the dining car window; one of his great delights was to see the English countryside from a train. It went back to his childhood when he used to travel, usually with his mother, to his grandmother's house in Wales. He remembered the thrill of seeing the great steam locomotive entering the station and climbing into the carriage which would take him to a different world. The sight of the engine belching steam and smoke, and the smell of soot that lingered in the air, came back vividly to Edwards. Then the English countryside used to turn into a precipitous track, high above the sea, through a series of tunnels, to the small, Welsh, university city.

The most exciting highlight of the trip for him was the great tubular railway bridge that they then rushed through. It had been designed by Stephenson and finished in 1850. On both sides of the bridge, stood two giant stone lions, that he always looked out for. It was then just a simple run across the flat, ancient peneplain of the island, and the local taxi from the railway station, to the isolated bungalow, high on a great rock, with its fabulous sea views, that was his grandmother's home. It had always been the centre of his solitary adventures during nearly all of his school holidays.

He awoke with a start from his childhood dreams. "Have you any questions?" demanded the fat man, his animal smells beginning to fill the room.

Edwards cleared his throat. "Yes," he said. "Can you tell me, please, why such attractive financial terms are made available and to what countries?"

The fat man observed him through half-closed eyes. "What I am about to tell you must never be repeated," he said. "These funds are made available to most developing countries by the American Government through an organisation in Langley, Virginia, called the Central Intelligence Agency."

Edwards shifted in his hard chair; as an avid reader of James Bond, he was well aware of this legendry intelligence organisation with its supposedly all-powerful grip on world affairs.

"So we are talking international politics?" Edwards asked carefully.

The fat man looked at him as if he was trying to deal with a child. "Of course," the man replied. "But every project the funds are used for has to be approved at the highest level, and we will only deal directly with certain people that have been cleared to deal with these matters. Potentially like yourself."

For the first time, the fat man smiled at him. Edwards nodded, but he was still far from certain about what he was being told. He was, as always, sceptical about everything. One of his favourite sayings, coined during his university days, while avidly studying Political Thought, had been "I used to be a Cynic, but now I don't believe in anything." This usually raised a laugh from those aware of this ancient Greek school of philosophy founded by Antisthenes. Edwards was, however, totally unaware of his hypocrisy; that ancient school had contempt for ease and pleasure, whereas Edwards revelled in both!

"So what happens now?" asked Edwards.

"You will need to be cleared to the next stage," said the fat man, handing Edwards a scrap of paper bearing a name and address. "I have your number on your card and I will call you when these people are prepared to meet you."

"I think it best if you deal with Mr. Jones, as you know him already," said Edwards as they shook hands. It was a relief to get out of the stuffy room and away from that unpleasant individual. He sat down on a bench and thought about the meeting. He did not like the man; he decided that in future he would just call him the Fat Man, as he had already forgotten his name.

The call of the cathedral was now very strong. But first, Edwards had to eat. He thought again just how pleasant it was being out of that small room with that sweaty individual! He found a sandwich bar and went inside; he purchased a ham and cheese and the inevitable cup of coffee. After he had eaten, he went to sit for a while again on the same bench overlooking the cathedral. Finally, when he was ready, he entered the great echoing space. The vaulted ceiling was still there, and it was still as magnificent as he had remembered it.

On the train back from Exeter, he read the papers that the Fat Man had given him. They were badly constructed; his nose wrinkled at the way they were written. He had always been careful about his written English. Maybe they had been written by an American or some person who was not as careful as he was with the English language? He sat musing; of course, a trip such as this required both a full English Breakfast and a three-course dinner. It was all on somebody else's expenses, anyway, and his normal routine had been put aside for this long train trip today.

The three courses over, the waiter brought him coffee. "Have you a Kümmel?" Edwards asked, knowing full well that this was usually stocked on a British Rail dining car. The sweet, colourless, German liqueur was brought to him in a small shot glass. They knew, at least, that it must be served ice cold, thought Edwards, as he sipped it appreciatively. He again got out the papers that the Fat Man had given him. They really failed to make any sense to him; he must have hard words with Jones in the morning.

# 3

The British Airways Trident rose slightly and then began its descent. Edwards sat in his comfortable business class seat by the window. He looked out carefully at the wings and the moveable spoilers, on their leading edge, which helped keep the aircraft in the air. Some ten years before, a Trident, on its way to Brussels from Heathrow, had crashed just after take-off, killing all on board. The pilot had retracted his spoilers too quickly.

For Edwards, the thrill of flying was now gone; he had been on too many trips abroad. Even the comfortable wait in the business class lounge and the full-on business, or sometimes even first class, cabin service, which he always enjoyed, did not make up for the boredom of flying and the usually early starts from home. But, this morning, the in-flight service had been excellent.

The stewardess had been particularly insistent. "A glass of Champagne with your breakfast, sir?" she had asked. Edwards had several; really the only way to start the day! He smiled to himself. It reminded him of the story of the millionaire British celebrity, who was once asked, on an American television chat-show, what his English Breakfast usually consisted of? When he mentioned that it consisted, along with the other expected ingredients, of a bottle of Champagne every morning, the female interviewer looked horrified. "For how long have you being doing that?" she asked. "For as long as I have been able to afford it," had been the instant reply.

Geneva Airport is unusual; it is probably the only airport in the world where you can decide which country you would like to arrive in. After leaving the aircraft, Edwards walked down the long corridor. At the end, there were two signs. To the left, he could arrive in France, and to the right, he would arrive in Switzerland. He took the right-hand turn and proudly presented his dark blue British passport to the Swiss official. Sometimes, during a long flight, he would take it out of his pocket and read the magnificent words printed behind the front cover. "Her Britannic Majesty's Principal Secretary of State for Foreign and Commonwealth Affairs Requests and requires in the Name of Her Majesty all those whom it may concern to allow the bearer to pass freely without let or hindrance, and to afford the bearer such assistance and protection as may be necessary."

The Jet d'Eau was pumping out its 100 gallons of water a second, up to over 400 feet, as his taxi passed along the busy road beside the lake. Edwards liked Geneva; in particular, he remembered a happy week some years ago that he and his wife had spent just along the lake in Montreux. It had been another warm June; he had spent his days in the basement of the Palais du Congress, manning a desk for his bank, at a top-level conference on the Arab world. She had been free to go, with the other wives, on various visits, including one he envied her to Zermatt, for a view of the Matterhorn. He had to pay for her flight, but at least the hotel and the food were on the company.

Each evening they had walked arm-in-arm together along the fashionable Promenade. It was the combination of the sparkling lake and the still snow-capped mountains behind it that had inspired Edwards. The air was fresh and invigorating, and he could have been a millionaire taking his new, pretty wife for a stroll before returning to their five-star hotel. In fact, the company had been mean; it was only a three-star hotel that they provided, but it was comfortable enough and the view from their tenth-floor room was spectacular. They had stayed on for the weekend, at their own expense, and made a romantic visit to the lakeside Chateau de Chillon.

Jones had been insistent; Edwards's first meeting must be followed up, and Marketing would pay for his day trip to Geneva. Jones had contacted the Fat Man, and a few days later, a date and time had been agreed. At the airport taxi rank, Edwards had shown the scrap of paper the Fat Man had given him, to the driver. He was in no doubt that it would be an expensive fare, but he had a wad of Swiss francs in his wallet, and it was not as if it was his money, was it? The taxi ended up in a back street that was several streets away from the lake. As he got out of the taxi and paid the driver, Edwards thought it was all rather dark and dismal.

The street number given on the scrap of paper was a nondescript block of apartments with a nondescript entrance. On the left-hand side of the door, Edwards carefully inspected several rows of bell pushes. By each button, a name had been carefully printed. Over one name, a small piece of paper had been temporarily attached with some sticky transparent tape; "de Winter" the hand-written name read. Edwards checked the name on the scrap of paper; it was the same. He pressed the bell. He was expected; a woman's voice answered. "Second floor," it said.

Edwards had to be quick with the heavy door as the lock buzzed open. Inside there was a chill in the air; the sun never penetrated to this cold, plain hallway. The walls were in a good decorative state: off-white emulsion with brown paint for the wooden fittings. He climbed the light brown, stone steps, wondering what awaited him. On the second landing, a door stood slightly open. He knocked and the door opened fully from the inside.

# 4

She was quite short and wore a grey and white dress. Edwards estimated that she was about fifty years old. He noticed that she had a good figure; her hair was dark but with flecks of grey which betrayed her age. "Monsieur Edwards?" she asked. She was not French. Like most Englishmen, Edwards had a trained ear for accents. He placed her perhaps from the German-speaking part of Switzerland. Before his marriage, Edwards had had the experience of a series of foreign girlfriends; one of them had been a tall, blonde Swiss girl from the north of Zurich. With her, he had travelled to most parts of Switzerland, learnt much about the country and seen a lot of its breath-taking scenery.

She led him down the narrow hallway into a living room; it was comfortably but rather fussily furnished with striped pale-coloured wallpaper. Its window looked out only onto the block of flats across the street. She guided Edwards to the soft sofa. "Would you like a coffee?" she asked. Edwards nodded; again he detected, to him, the unmistakable Schweizerdeutsch accent. From the piece of paper stuck by the bell push, he had concluded that this was not her home. The flat had merely been borrowed for this meeting. She had now left the room and Edwards sat there wondering what was going to happen next? A tall, rather stooping man entered; he had fine grey hair, slightly receding from his temples. Despite himself, Edwards was impressed. The man wore an impeccable three-piece suit with a sober shirt and tie. His black, well-burnished shoes looked handmade.

In the same accent as his wife, he introduced himself. Edwards had to assume that they were a married couple, as she was now back in the comfortable living room with a tray of hot drinks. There was coffee for Edwards, as requested, and he caught the familiar smell of the Earl

Grey tea, without milk, that she gave to her husband. He handed de Winter his business card; the man put it down on the coffee table in front of him and observed it carefully. He did not proffer his card in return. His grey eyes seemed to bore through Edwards, and then he asked the usual required pleasantries about his journey and whether his flight had been on time?

Edwards loosened up; for some reason, he began to feel comfortable with this Swiss couple he had only just met. The wife returned with a plate of excellent Swiss biscuits, and for Edwards, always concerned about his food, the day had certainly improved. They talked for over two hours; the husband was very knowledgeable about world affairs, and Edwards found their conversation entertaining. The wife said nothing, but sat there appearing to be interested in what the two men were saying. Suddenly, she disappeared, to return shortly with several plates of home-made sandwiches, more biscuits and a refill for Edwards's coffee cup. Edwards could only assume that the sandwiches had been made that morning, ready for this meeting.

De Winter knew little about the operation of "the Fund" as he called it, but he did cite several large projects in various countries, where the Fund had been involved in the financing. When asked by Edwards whether he had been personally involved in any project, de Winter mentioned a major hotel and shopping centre that he had helped design and build in Tanzania. There the Fund had provided finance for twenty years at a fixed three per cent interest rate in an amount of seventy-five million United States dollars. Like all Swiss, he was very precise about money; the Government of Tanzania had supported the project, but not with a guarantee. The Fund had decided, exceptionally, to take the private sector risk on the project, secured by a mortgage on the buildings.

Edwards listened carefully; for the first time, he was getting some of the details he craved. De Winter turned to him; "I am only a humble architect," he said. "What you must do is to meet Herr Doctor Sanders."

Edwards liked the Germanic habit of giving people their full and correct titles. "Is he a practising medical practitioner?" he asked and then hoped that de Winter would understand this rather unusual English term.

But he need not have worried; a slight smile came over de Winter's face as he said something that he thought was very important.

"Herr Doctor Sanders is a graduate of Yale University. His Doctorate is in Modern History, and he is a Senior Adviser to the American Central Intelligence Agency."

After that announcement, there was not much more; de Winter sat at the desk against one wall of the room and with an expensive-looking fountain pen, wrote down on an expensive piece of paper, the contact details for Herr Doctor Sanders. He passed it to Edwards, who appeared suitably grateful. They shook hands and Edwards thanked his wife, rather profusely, for the excellent sandwiches.

The trip back was routine; he walked down to the main road beside the lake and hailed another taxi to the airport. On the aircraft back to London, Edwards thought about the day. It already seemed rather unreal; the temporarily borrowed flat, the charming Swiss couple and the rather erudite conversation with de Winter. He fell asleep after he had eaten his business class dinner and did not wake up until after the aircraft had started its descent into Heathrow Airport.

# 5

The taxi driver must have thought that he had wanted a sightseeing tour; he had been given a good view of the Eiffel Tower and they were now competing with the traffic around the Arc de Triomphe before plunging down the Champs-Élysées. It was now late June, but Paris was still full. The locals had not yet left with their families for their country homes or their cheap hotels and camping sites by the sea. This they would do in mid-July, once the school holidays had started. At Charles de Gaulle Airport, he had done his usual thing of showing the taxi driver the expensive piece of paper that de Winter had given him.

The address was in the 6<sup>th</sup> Arrondissement, and he had contacted the telephone number he had been given a few days before. A girl had answered, first in French but, when she had realised that the call was from London, in perfect English. An appointment had been set with Doctor Sanders at his office for this afternoon at two o'clock Paris time. With the time difference and the need to arrive at the airport well before his flight, this had meant another early start for Edwards, and he was not at all pleased by that.

Jones had been delighted by Edwards's report of his visit to Geneva. In retrospect, Edwards even felt that he was at last getting somewhere, and therefore, he had readily agreed to a visit to Paris, again with the Marketing Department budget taking the strain.

As he bounced around in the back of the taxi, Edwards thought about his several previous visits to this city. Years before, in his stock-broking days, he had come here with Philip. Philip had been his dealing colleague; he was rumoured to take home an enormous salary, mostly based on his annual bonus, and to have a limitless expense account. They had stayed luxuriously at the Hotel Georges Cinque; Edwards had always joked afterwards that the unusual extra tap in his en-suite bathroom, which he knew was to provide a salt water bath, was actually for Champagne! In the evening, Philip had introduced him to the tasteful delights of the Crazy Horse Saloon, and they had then ended up in a nightclub in the Pigalle district. Edwards thought back to the beautiful faces of the two high-class prostitutes, whom Philip had invited over to their table.

For Edwards, it had all been rather embarrassing; the blond girl had fastened on to Philip and the brunette had started talking to him. Without bidding, the waiter had brought a bottle of overpriced Champagne in an ice bucket and some glasses. "For the ladies," he had muttered. The brunette was beautiful; she tossed her long hair as she spoke to Edwards in perfect English. Her low-cut white sparkling dress was made to reveal her fulsome breasts. She told Edwards that she was a student at the Sorbonne and only came to this nightclub to meet nice men to help pay her fees at university. She crossed her long legs and leaned towards him. Her beautiful brown eyes seemed to bore into his soul. She spoke to him softly and then put her hand on his leg. Leaning further forward, she whispered into his ear, "There are some bedrooms upstairs. Would you like to go up?"

Edwards was both fascinated and terrified. Then he had not been married, but he had slept with several of his girlfriends. In matters of sex, however, he was really a bit of a puritan. The thought of paying for sex frankly appalled him. Edwards glanced towards Philip; he was holding the hand of his girl and then they kissed. Philip stood up. "Just going upstairs with this lovely," he said in his half-Cockney accent. The blond followed him, her hips swinging lasciviously. Edwards had to make it clear to his girl that he did not want to take advantage of this opportunity. She had seemed disappointed. "Let's just sit and talk," he had said.

When Philip came back, he looked suitably refreshed. Embarrassed, Edwards explained that he "did not feel up to it tonight." Philip had just laughed, produced a great wad of French franc notes, paid the waiter for their drinks and then shared out the remaining money between the two girls. In the taxi back to the hotel, a curious Edwards asked him how he had enjoyed it?

"Just like screwing my wife," replied Philip, with a big grin on his face.

"But what about all that money you gave them?" asked Edwards.

Philip laughed. "I'll just stick it on my expenses for entertaining," he said. "It certainly entertained me!"

# 6

The building was grey, long and low; it had probably been built in the 1950s and was out of keeping with the rest of the buildings in the street. On the ground floor were some small shops and a Post Office. Above, there might have been either offices or apartments. Edwards paid his taxi driver off and then walked past the building. He always liked to carry out an inspection first, before entering any unknown building. During his reconnaissance, he noticed, at the far end of the building, an entrance with the number of the building above it.

He entered and saw, sitting behind an old, rather broken-down desk, a fit-looking, young man. By his dress, manner and appearance, Edwards instantly recognised him as an American. The man stood up as Edwards approached; he was over six foot tall, fit and lean. The muscles rippled beneath his rather creased suit. The words "American Special Forces" came into Edwards's mind; he had met a few men like this in the City. Still very fit, well-educated and intelligent; they could "turn their hand" to practically anything. They had retired from the Armed Forces early, but would only speak obliquely of their time in Hereford with the Special Air Service.

"Can I help you, sir?" The voice was cultured. East Coast, probably New England, Edwards thought.

"I have an appointment with Doctor Sanders," said Edwards.

"Your name, please, sir?" It was not a request, it was a command.

Edwards gave his name and, when asked, his passport for inspection. The young man then asked to see inside the briefcase that Edwards carried with him. "I have to give you a quick pat-down now, sir," said the bodyguard, for that was what he was.

Edwards stood up straight, with his arms outstretched, as the guard very expertly checked that he was not carrying any kind of concealed weapon. "Office number four on the first floor, sir," said the guard. Edwards climbed the stairs and then turned right down the corridor. Each office was numbered; number four was only the second on the right. He knocked and heard a voice from inside. He entered.

The office was larger than Edwards had expected, but it was sparsely furnished; just a desk, two chairs and a metal filing cabinet. The carpet seemed to be the same grey colour as the outside of the building. The only decoration was a Pirelli Calendar on one wall. It was for the current year and opened for the right month. Behind the desk sat a man; he rose as Edwards entered. He was shorter than the guard downstairs, but just as lean and fit. He was also older than the guard; his dark hair was swept back from a craggy face and a granite jaw. His black eyes pierced straight through Edwards and seemed to see and understand everything about him in just one moment.

"Doctor Sanders? I am Edwards from London." He extended his hand to the stranger and received a very firm handshake.

"Good Afternoon, Mr. Edwards. Thank you for coming," the man replied. There was a slight Texan drawl. Sanders indicated that he could sit down, and Edwards handed him his business card. For the first time on this pilgrimage, he received one back. It bore the name of "the Fund" and an address in Washington. Edwards knew where the street was; it was not far from the White House. "Dr. George J. Sanders lll" was printed on the card and beneath the name the words "Chief Executive Officer." Edwards did not like the habit of some Americans of giving exactly the same name to their children and grandchildren and then adding numbers to differentiate them as if they were a Royal House. Strangely, there was no telephone number printed on the card.

"I believe that you have met my associates in Geneva, Mr. Edwards," growled the Texan. "They have sent me a good report on you and your company. I believe that we can do business together."

Edwards had not expected this simple acceptance and was rather lost for words. But he recovered quickly. "Perhaps we can talk about a specific project?" he asked.

"Sure," growled the Texan. Edwards spoke about the project that he and Jones had carefully selected to "test out" the Fund. It was a bank building, under construction in the centre of Cairo, which Jones's construction company had taken over from a failed Egyptian contractor. The building was in a mess, but it needed to be completed. The Egyptian bank, which would occupy and own it, was one of the top four banks in Egypt, but it did not want to give out any more cash. Instead, it wanted to guarantee a long-term loan of sixty million dollars to provide the money to finish the building. Would this be possible?

The Texan asked a few questions, which Edwards easily answered. He obviously knew about projects and building them, thought Edwards. "A formal application to the Fund will be necessary, Mr. Edwards, but I can give you the form now." The Texan opened a drawer in his desk and took out some papers in a transparent plastic folder. He handed them to Edwards. Edwards did not look at them; he could not read and listen at the same time. He was by now rather fascinated by this American who only used one word when most people would have used three or four!

"In principle, it sounds fine to me," said the American. "There will, of course, be an Application Fee of two hundred and fifty thousand good old United States dollars. We use this to defray some of our expenses, and to separate out the serious borrowers and the serious projects. You can imagine that, with the kind of lending terms we offer, there is a very high demand. We do not want to waste our time or yours, Mr. Edwards."

Edwards nodded; he understood that an American like this would not want to waste his time. The Texan rose from his chair and so did Edwards. He extended his hand and Edwards shook it warmly. "You will find all the instructions with the Application Form," said the Texan. "A safe journey back to London." Edwards found himself back on the pavement outside the grey building. It took him half an hour to find a passing, vacant taxi, with its taxi light illuminated, but then it did not stop when he hailed it.

He was getting flustered and afraid that he would miss his flight; he had started to sweat. There were just no taxis around! Suddenly a taxi stopped on the other side of the street. A well-dressed woman got out. Risking life and limb, Edwards dashed across the street. He made a grab to open the back door of the taxi and jumped in, before the woman had time to even finish paying her fare. "Aeroport Charles de Gaulle!" he shouted rudely at the taxi driver.

# 7

For some reason, Edwards was worried; he was very worried. But he did not know why. His aircraft had been delayed for two hours and he had to hang around the airport. He had spent so much on taxis that he did not want to spend more on dinner at the various food outlets, even though some of them looked good. He settled for several "free" drinks and snacks in the business class lounge. At least he had somewhere comfortable to sit and newspapers to read while the mob outside tried to find just a place to sit down. At last, he was on the aircraft and it had taken off. He ravenously ate the business class dinner on offer. He did not get home until very late. He let himself in; his wife had locked the mortice lock and was already asleep in their bed.

Back in the office the next morning, his worry did not leave him. Something was wrong, very wrong. He went back over the events and the conversation of the previous day. His visit to Paris already seemed a long time ago. He had met with Jones straight away in the morning. This time, he did not have to go to Jones's office; Jones came to his. Jones was delighted. "Let me take the forms and start filling them in," he requested.

"No. I want to read them properly first," said Edwards. He closed his office door and sat behind his desk just thinking. What was it that was worrying him?

Suddenly it hit him! The American had asked for two hundred and fifty thousand dollars up-front! An Application Fee, he had called it. But Edwards had really been unable to find out anything much about the American organisation. The Texan had assured Edwards that "in principle" things should go ahead and they would get their loan. But what if this did not happen? He had already spent lots of his group's money on travelling around, or, at least, Jones had. Yes, he could blame Jones. But then he was the financial expert, and they would all blame him if anything went wrong! There seemed no escape.

He realised that he had been a fool; why had he not asked the American more about his organisation? But then he would not know whether he had been told the truth? How could you verify such an organisation existed except to fly to Washington and go to their building? To actually see their offices was the only way. What about asking to speak to someone whom they had already financed? But how would he know, even then, that he would be told the truth? Two hundred and fifty thousand dollars! That was quite a small sum in relation to the total cost of the Egyptian project, but it was still over four times his annual salary! What a fool he had been getting himself into this business and allowing Jones to persuade him to go on all these trips.

He took the papers the American had given him out of his desk and spent a full thirty minutes examining them. The Application Form was straight forward enough. But there was nothing in the papers about the Fund. He then remembered what the Fat Man had said; it was the American Government fronted up by the Central

Intelligence Agency. De Winter had said that Sanders was a Senior Adviser to them. But you could not just telephone the C.I.A. and ask them, "Was Doctor George J. Sanders the Third a Senior Adviser to your organisation?" The only other piece of paper in the plastic folder was an instruction on how to pay the Application Fee. It was to be sent, at the same time as the Application Form was posted to their Washington office, by Telegraphic Transfer to a bank account in Panama!

Before he went home that night, he took the papers out and read them again. Then, on impulse, he pushed them quickly into his briefcase. At least he could hide them at home. But then Jones would demand to see them tomorrow. What was he to do? It was a long, slow drive home that evening; the traffic was as bad as usual, but it had all seemed even more frustrating. He had a miserable evening; he did not even watch the television but sat in front of the set, not even conscious of what was on. His dinner had been tasteless and he hardly spoke to his wife. His mind was churning over the vast problem that he now seemed to have. Then he remembered the Swiss couple; he had liked them. He recalled de Winter's words; the Fund had financed a project for him. But where had it been? Oh yes, in Tanzania.

# 8

That night he could not sleep. His mind was in a maelstrom; first one, then an alternative and then a third in a series of possibilities came into his febrile brain. Was the American for real? Was de Winter part of their conspiracy or was he just an honest man that was a potential victim, too? He did not even think about the Fat Man. He tossed and turned. Fortunately for him, his wife was a heavy sleeper and did not seem to be disturbed. It was about three o'clock in the morning when he eventually fell asleep. At six o'clock, as usual, his clock radio woke him up; he always listened to the BBC World Service News at this time. Dealing with so many countries, he had to listen to it every morning, including at the weekends. He could not afford to miss any important international news item.

But this morning the radio was not welcome. At six-thirty, he staggered out of bed as his wife woke up. He had his usual breakfast; two wheat biscuits with milk, a cup of weak tea and then a cup of strong coffee. He shaved, showered and did the other business! He climbed into the car; the usual long, stop-start journey ground him down further. Usually, his brain helped him to solve any problems overnight; often, he had been amazed when he was able to come to a solution in the morning after "he had slept on it." But not this time; this time it was just too difficult.

When he got to the office, he sat behind his desk trying to think. Liz brought in his first mug of coffee. "Thanks, Liz," he managed to say. "Close the door please, and if you have a Do Not Disturb sign, hang it up." This touch of humour pleased him, but his head was throbbing and his eyes kept on closing. In desperation, he fixed his gaze on his "Worry Picture."

He stared at Monet's calm water. His lack of sleep, worry and stress must have been making him hallucinate. The water lilies were becoming detached from the surface of the water and beginning to float towards him! Suddenly a face appeared; he recognised it. That was unusual for Edwards as normally he had difficulty in bringing faces and names together. It was Simon, one of the insurance brokers he used to help him offset, at a price, some of the risks his companies faced operating in difficult and sometimes dangerous countries.

Instinctively he reached to open the bottom left-hand drawer of his desk.

Inside that drawer were some twenty-five black folders; inside each were business cards, presented to him by other people, neatly filed between thick transparent plastic pages. Sometimes he collected so many cards that he filled one of these folders in a month; at other times it was not so busy. Every few months, Liz went out and bought him some more folders as the group's Stationary Department did not stock them. Then she carefully put a sticky label at the front of each full folder, detailing the month or months over which the cards inside had been collected.

He went through last month's folder without success. He opened the previous one and started to go through the pages. There it was! Simon was only a manager, but such was the importance of Edwards's group, that two months ago, Simon had arranged for Edwards to have lunch at his insurance broking firm. It was a large and well-established firm and had plush offices in the City of London. On the top floor were some executive dining rooms, and here Edwards had been entertained to a very good City lunch.

As well as Simon, who was his main contact, there had been three directors of the firm present. After the third course, an excellent dessert, coffee had been brought and port, brandy and cigars had been served by three waiters, there to cater to their every need. Edwards had chosen the port; fortunately, he remembered the right hand to use in passing the port bottle the right way around the table. He had also helped himself to a large Havana cigar; a type which he occasionally enjoyed.

He had found the cards of the three directors who had entertained him. One came into his mind; a tall, distinguished gentleman with a magnificent head of wavy white hair. He had worn an impeccable three-piece City suit. He had not said very much, but had listened carefully to everything that Edwards had said. Edwards found his card. Between the name of Simon's broking firm at the top, and its address and telephone number at the bottom, was written his name. "Charles Bartlett CMG, Director."

Edwards knew what CMG meant; the civil servants, he sometimes worked closely with, called it irreverently the "Call Me God!" The rank of Companion of The Most Distinguished Order of Saint Michael and Saint George was awarded by the Queen to some senior Diplomats and Foreign Office civil servants when they had reached a sufficient seniority or when they retired from service in the Foreign and Commonwealth Office.

Simon had come to Edwards's office some two weeks later; his aim was to follow up on the potential insurance business for his firm that had been discussed at the lunch. After a ninety minute discussion on a number of difficult cases, Simon got up to leave.

"What did you think of old Bartlett?" he asked Edwards, almost as an afterthought.

"He was rather quiet," answered Edward, who sometimes liked too much the sound of his own voice.

"That's his background," said Simon. "We recruited him after he retired because of his inside knowledge of so many parts of the world and the fact that he can get up to date again, if he wants to, by talking to his former colleagues."

"Where was he?" enquired Edwards always interested in the international world.

"The people over on the South Bank," said Simon. "For those in the know, they are called the "Friends.""

Edwards looked blank; he did not understand what Simon was talking about. But Simon quickly explained to him what the secretive organisation was, funded through the Foreign and Commonwealth Office, where Bartlett had enjoyed such a long and distinguished career.

# 9

Edwards picked up the receiver of his direct line telephone; in front of him was Simon's card extracted from the card index on his desk, which was sorted by Liz into strict alphabetical order. He dialled the number on the card. After five rings, Simon answered. Edwards did not want to tell him the real story; he would have felt a complete fool to tell him what had happened. Instead, he said to him that he had a problem that maybe Charles Bartlett could help with. He hinted that it was of a highly confidential nature. Simon understood immediately and wanted to help his important, potential client. He said that he would ask Charles to call him. "On the direct line, please," asked Edwards and reminded Simon of the number. He did not want any of these kinds of calls going through to the telephone operators downstairs.

He still felt terrible; he tried to do some other work, but he could hardly do anything. He asked Liz to switch all his calls to her telephone except for those on the direct line and say that he was away from the office that morning. She was sympathetic. "Is there anything I can do?" she asked.

I feel terrible," said Edwards. "I think I must have some kind of flu."

"Aspirin?" asked Liz.

"Oh, do go out and get me some please," said Edwards.

"No need," said the ever-helpful Liz. "I have some in my desk."

He waited for the call; he stared out of the window at the constant traffic on the flyover. He wondered about the lives of the people who were driving past. Did any of them have such a complicated job to do as he had? He was very well paid and had a "top-of-the-range" company car, but did that really make up for the stress of his job and driving in every working day to this office? At twelve-fifteen his direct line rang; he snatched it up. "Edwards," he answered.

The quiet, cultivated voice at the other end of the line said, "This is Charles Bartlett. Simon has asked me to give you a call."

Edwards made a complete hash of telling Bartlett what had happened. He gave a long and rather confused story of the events and the three meetings that he had attended over the last three weeks or so. At the end, his voice just dried up. There was a silence; to Edwards, it seemed to last for a whole minute. In fact, it only lasted for some five seconds. "I will get someone to call you," said Bartlett. Then the line went dead.

Edwards had a good lunch in the executive canteen; he always believed that food could help in any difficult situation. This, combined with the Aspirin and the supply of coffee from Liz, helped him to feel better. Liz had asked to leave early that day; her mother was arriving from Yorkshire to stay with her and she wanted to meet her at Euston Station. Edwards sat behind his desk still trying to do some work. Now Liz had left and switched his other line through again. There were sometimes stupid calls to answer coming from some of his colleagues. "Why do people never listen properly?"

thought Edwards. "And why do they never do what they said that they were going to do?" But, at least, it made him forget, for the moment, his problems.

At four-thirty his direct line rang; he snatched it up. "Edwards," he answered. What was said on the other end of the line electrified him; he sat bolt upright in his chair. The voice was that of a young man, but he was confident, cultivated and laconic. Edwards had heard the same accent before from some of his former upper-class banking colleagues. He knew that the man on the other end of the line had attended one of the oldest and most expensive public schools in Britain. Located to the west of London, near Windsor, and founded in 1440, it had supplied, over the centuries, most of the leading British statesmen. The education provided by this establishment, led on to a unique set of contacts and to some of the highest positions in the land.

"Foreign and Commonwealth Office here. Permanent Secretary's Department speaking. I understand that you have been talking to Charles Bartlett." No name was given, but Edwards knew instinctively, that you could not expect to be given the name of one of the employees of the government's international Secret Intelligence Service. This time, he told his story in a far more logical and properly constructed way. The young man at the other end of the line only listened; he asked no questions. When Edwards had clearly finished his tale, the man simply said, "I will make some enquiries. I will revert to you within twenty-four hours." Then the line went dead.

# 10

It was as if a great weight had come off his chest. He had spoken to someone who really might be able to help him. But could he and would he? The worries started to come back again as Edwards drove home. That evening, he helped himself to a third gin and tonic; he had forgotten that he had already drunk two. "I think that you are beginning to drink too much," said his wife.

That night, he had slept better. In the morning, he got up as soon as his clock radio came on. He wanted to get to the office early in case the man from the Foreign Office called him. For some reason, the traffic seemed better. It was a sunny and warm day at the end of June. He got to his office and sat down behind his desk. Liz brought in his first mug of coffee. "Mr. Jones of Marketing has been trying to get hold of you," she said. Jones! What was he going to tell Jones? He decided to tell him nothing until he had heard back from the Public School Boy, as he now called him. He thought about the exact words he might use to Jones.

At about ten-thirty his internal telephone line rang; he picked it up. It was Jones. "Can I have those papers, please?" he asked. Edwards explained that he had still not finished with them.

"But we must get on," said Jones. "We cannot keep these important people waiting."

"I have got some enquiries out on them at the moment," responded Edwards.

"Who have you spoken to?" was Jones's simple question.

Edwards thought quickly. "I am afraid that I cannot tell you," he said. "I have a confidential source that I sometimes use."

After that exchange with Jones, he felt rather smug; somehow he had put the man back in his place. After all, it was Jones who had sent him off on what increasingly looked to be "a fool's errand." But what if the Public School Boy came back with a positive answer? What if he confirmed that Doctor George Sanders was an Adviser to the Central Intelligence Agency? Would he even do that? Was such confidential, no, secret, information ever given to a mere mortal such as himself? The Public School Boy might just fob him off with something that did not prove anything either way. What would Edwards do then? What would he tell Jones? Even more importantly, what would he tell the director to whom he reported?

He fretted anew about the intolerable situation in which he found himself. If only he had been stronger and told Jones, straight away, that this great pilgrimage to find this "Manna from Heaven" was doomed from the start. It was all such an unlikely story that he could have dismissed it straight away. After all, he was the financial expert! All through the rest of the morning, he waited for his direct line to ring; frustratingly, it remained silent. Lunchtime came and he went to have lunch in the executive canteen. Everybody around him seemed to be jolly. His colleagues were commenting to each other that it was such a nice day and that the weather was set fair for the weekend. Only then, did he realise that it was Friday. He had even forgotten what day of the week it was!

He returned to his desk; he tried to busy himself with some papers. But again, he could not concentrate. There were only a few telephone calls to answer; it was already Friday afternoon and he realised that many people would soon be leaving early for the weekend. Liz came in with another mug of coffee. "Can you keep the door closed, please Liz?" he asked. At three-thirty precisely, his direct line rang. He grabbed the receiver of the telephone. "Edwards," he answered.

It was the same voice; the intonation was that of the class that naturally ruled the country. "I have carried out some enquiries with our Cousins," the voice said. "The results are as follows." Edwards grabbed a pad of paper and a pen. He scribbled furiously as he noted down verbatim what he was being told. Afterwards, he read it back again and again to try and absorb the full impact of the words he had written down.

"First, the building that you visited in Paris was an outstation of the American Agency up to eighteen months ago. It is no longer. Second, the organisation that you mentioned in Washington does not exist. Third, Doctor George Sanders is not and never has been an employee of, or an Adviser to, the American Agency."

Edwards had difficulty in stopping himself from shouting out loud, with joy! He thanked the young man profusely. "Not at all," came the reply. "We try to help where we can. If there is any other appropriate matter in the future, do speak to Charles Bartlett. Charles is still very well thought of here." Then the line went dead.

Edwards fell forward onto his desk. It was just as if a noose had been around his neck, slowing strangling him, and it had suddenly been cut. He now knew it had all been a complex confidence trick to steal two hundred and fifty thousand United States dollars from his group of companies. It was a major, attempted fraud of international dimensions.

He now knew also what he would say to Jones; but he would not do it until Monday. He was too tired to confront Jones immediately. "Sorry, but my confidential sources have told me, that the organisation in Washington does not exist. They suspect that this is just a clever confidence trick, a fraud, to get the Application Fee from us. We would never see that money again, or get any funds to finance our project." He would say all of this to Jones, and that would be the end of the matter.

Liz entered his office and looked at him. "Are you alright?" she asked, as always, concerned about him. Edwards sat up and smiled at her.

"Yes, I am fine, thanks!" he replied. "I think that the weather is going to be good for the weekend." He leaned back in his comfortable executive chair. He was now looking forward to his weekend; he was certainly going to enjoy it!

THE END

# The Banker

-

*"One who deceives, will always find those,
who allow themselves to be deceived."*

— **Niccolò Machiavelli**

# 1

The speedboat rode quietly on the fast-flowing ebb tide. Two ropes had been tied to the scaffolding, put up to help repair the bridge, which loomed over the boat. The bridge had been opened in 1869 by the then Queen, who had gone on to reign for another thirty-two years before her death at the age of eighty-one. The ropes were there to try and keep the boat steady. The bow of the boat was well under the massive structure and pointed down-river, and there was one man at the wheel to try and keep the boat stationary. It was the early hours of the morning on a warm June night, and the boat's engine had been turned off, to try and avoid discovery. But the boat was so well hidden under the bridge, and the jutting scaffolding, that nobody could see it.

Three more men were standing at the stern of the boat, facing in the direction from which the boat had come. Two, like the man at the wheel, were dressed entirely in black. They had changed from their business suits, which they had worn earlier, to collect the fourth man from his flat in a fashionable part of this city. They had bundled him into a car, borrowed from their local accomplice who, of course, had asked no questions.

The fourth man was dressed in an impeccable, three-piece, business suit; he was smaller than the others and rather overweight. The pockets of his suit bulged with the bricks and the wads of money that had been thrust into them. A line of perspiration was on his forehead and his eyes stared wildly. His impeccably burnished black handmade shoes gleamed even in the dim light. The state of these shoes would become a major point of discussion in the enquiries which would go on for many years afterwards. How was it that he had scrambled over the dusty scaffolding, without any trace of dust being found on his shoes?

His hands were tied with a slip knot that could easily be pulled away, and the same slip knot had been tied around his ankles. He was not gagged, but he had been warned, in no uncertain terms, that, if he made any noise, his family would be exterminated.

It was the dead of night; the city was quiet. Traffic had even stopped flowing over the bridge above the boat. Either side of the bridge, on both banks of the river, the lights of the huge city twinkled. Hanging perpendicularly down was another rope; it was also tied to the scaffolding. At the other end, a simple noose had been made, which had been put around the fourth man's neck and pulled tight.

It would be a slow and painful death from asphyxiation as the tide flowed out and the boat dropped down with the ebbing water. Not like the normal death by hanging that he was used to, thought the senior of the three men dressed all in black. He had arranged for that to happen several times before. That was a quick killing, as the neck of the victim had just snapped, as he had kicked away the chair that he had used for them to stand on.

Their orders had been to make this death look like suicide, but to make it as difficult for this victim as possible. This man had to be fully paid back for his heinous crimes. Soon the revenge of the Brotherhoods of the former members of the now-dissolved, secret Masonic Lodge known as Propaganda Due and the organisation called Cosa Nostra, which had employed him and his colleagues, and which remained very much alive and powerful, would, at last, be completed.

An hour later, after making sure that the now hanging man was dead, the two men in the stern quickly pulled the ropes away from his hands and from his ankles. The two ropes attaching the speedboat to the scaffolding, surrounding that part of the bridge, were untied and the engine started. The boat had been purchased, just two days ago, for cash, from a boatyard much further up the river. It had been bought by the man now at the wheel, who knew something about boats. It was third-hand and rather dilapidated, so he had inspected the engine carefully. It would soon be scuttled and sunk in deep water in the wide estuary just before the river reached the sea.

After that, the three men would change and dress casually to look like seamen. They would then take passage home, as part of the crew, on the small freighter that, even now, was moored downriver, at the large port complex, that served this capital city and its surrounding country.

# 2

It was some eight years earlier, in 1974. Four men were being shown to their table, by the head waiter, in what was a first-class restaurant. The walls of the restaurant were covered with oak panels; from the ceiling hung numerous fine candelabra. The tables were spaced far enough apart to allow for the total privacy of the diners. These diners mostly consisted of men dressed in expensive, business suits. But, occasionally, there was a smaller table with a similarly dressed, usually older man, sitting opposite a younger, beautiful, expensively dressed woman.

The lighted candelabra sparkled off the jewellery worn by this small number of women, who knew that they were not only the centre of attention for their wealthy lovers, but were also lusted after by most of the men in the room. The strong daylight from the large windows, also shone off the silver cutlery and fine cut glass, placed neatly on the starched white tablecloths, on each of the tables.

The party arrived at the table specially booked for their lunch. One of the seats was set against the wall. Above it was a plaque decorated with scrolls, and above that was a large Italian flag, its pole was inserted into a bracket fastened on to the wall. Edwards could not read what was written on the plaque; he had only a few words of Italian. "We will put you in Cavour's seat," said the bank Director to Edwards.

Fortunately, Edwards knew who Cavour was; at university, one of his papers had been on Modern European Political History. Camillo Benso, Count of Cavour, had, for less than three months, been the first Prime Minister of a united Italy before he had tragically died. He had been the main politician, who had worked tirelessly to make the numerous, independent, Italian city-states join together. But, crucially, he had been supported by Giuseppe Garibaldi, the great soldier and nationalist, who had fought with his army, until all resistance to the idea of a new united nation had crumbled, and the United Kingdom of Italy had been declared in 1861.

"I am honoured to sit in the seat of the great Cavour," said Edwards, as the waiter pulled the table out from the wall a little, so that he could slide easily into his seat. His hosts joined him; they were a Director of one of the oldest banks in Italy and two of his senior colleagues. The Istituto Bancario San Paolo di Torino had been founded in 1563 when a Brotherhood known as the Compagnia di San Paolo had laid the foundations for what, a few years later, would become the Monte de Pieta. This new institution offered loans, at extremely low interest rates, to provide the poor with an alternative to usury.

"Cavour sat here so that he could see the new Italian Parliament building through the window," the Director informed Edwards. Edwards looked; across the great Piazza Castello, he could see the ornate Baroque building that had once been a royal palace, before it had become the first parliament of the newly united country. For only a short time, Turin had been the first capital city of the new country, before that privilege had moved to Florence and then, finally, to Rome.

It had been a magnificent meal; Edwards had asked for his favourite aperitif before the lunch. Appropriately, he had thought, Campari with tonic water. He had chosen a real Italian tomato soup to begin with and then Ossobuco served with the vegetables of the day. This was complemented by the fine Italian red wine, chosen by his hosts, after some deliberation between them. In addition, of course, there was a plentiful supply of bottled, sparkling, Pellegrino water. The finish was the best Zabaglione that Edwards had ever tasted. Along with the excellent coffee, he accepted, on the Director's recommendation, an Amaretto, a sweet, Italian liqueur, made out of almonds. From the proffered box on wheels, he accepted a large Havana cigar and let the waiter expertly prepare and then light it for him.

He was deeply moved by this most generous hospitality; he felt that he should do something to try and repay his hosts. As his international experience increased, he was slowly becoming a diplomat. He thought quickly and then he stood up. "I would like to propose a toast," he said. His hosts stood up as well. Edwards raised his wine glass, where there was still a little wine left. "To Cavour, Garibaldi and a United Italy," he said. They drank the toast. Edwards noticed that the Director's eyes had misted over.

"I would like to propose a toast too," the Director said. They remained standing. "To Her Majesty the Queen, and to our greatest ally, the United Kingdom," was the toast of the bank Director.

# 3

Only twelve months earlier, almost to the day, Edwards had been walking through the City of London. He had on his City uniform; a smart two-piece, business suit with a clean, well-ironed, white shirt and a sober tie. He wore well-burnished black shoes; only black shoes can be worn in the City, he had been firmly told.

By now, Edwards knew the City well; he had already worked there for over three years. He was proud to have achieved his position in what he felt, was the centre of the financial world. He knew that the City of London consisted of only one square mile; it included the area of the original London, established by the Celts and then developed by the Romans. In parts of the City, the original Roman walls could still be seen, and some of the streets bore strange names, testifying to their original use or because they once ended in a fortified gate that gave entry to this civilised enclave.

From Medieval times, the City had been a semi-autonomous city-state. It had its own Lord Mayor and Council with substantial powers and its own police force to maintain law and order. It boasted many ancient privileges and had become, since the establishment in the 13th century of the first goldsmiths and bankers, who had emigrated from Northern Italy, the centre of London's financial industries. The name of one of its main streets, Lombard Street, testified to this original link with Italy.

"It is a strange thing to know something that nobody else knows," thought Edwards to himself, as he walked. If the crowds around him had known his secret, one or some of them might well have attacked and robbed him.

He had reached the great junction of streets known as the Bank; on his right, stood the great fortress of the Bank of England. During his university days, Edwards had received the rare privilege of a guided tour of this building. He knew that there was a deep well in the internal courtyard of the building and that a store of food was always kept inside. In an emergency, the great doors could be slammed shut and the building could hold out for days. Every night, a picket of armed soldiers were stationed in the Bank; they had been dispatched to guard the Bank every evening since the Gordon Riots of 1780.

To his left stood the Mansion House, the ceremonial home of the Lord Mayor of the City of London. Edwards had visited there, too, during his special university tour which had been offered to try and encourage students to join the financial services industries, in which the City specialised. He remembered the fine buffet lunch, with wine. that they had been offered in the opulent surroundings of the Mansion House.

Edwards carefully crossed a number of roads, waiting each time for the "Green Man" to appear on each set of traffic lights. He knew that he could not afford, today, to have an accident.

He started to walk down Cheapside towards one of the banks at its end; he knew that this street had been named after the open-air market that had, for centuries, been held there. He swung the briefcase he was carrying carefully. It was now a rather battered briefcase that he had bought when he had first left home for university. It was now empty except for a large, brown paper envelope. Sealed inside this envelope was a thick wad of large denomination Bearer Bonds, as good as cash, to the total value of three hundred million United States dollars!

Edwards well knew that Bearer Bonds were what they said they were; like banknotes, they belonged to and were payable to the "bearer", the person who actually held them in their hand. They were an easily transferable source of wealth and totally untraceable. They were issued by countries or by major companies, in various currencies, and were evidence of money loaned by the original lender. Each bond usually had a series of coupons attached, by which the bearer, could claim a fixed, stated amount of interest, usually on an annual basis, paid free of any tax, from the banks listed on each coupon.

When they matured, after the stated period of the loan, the principle sum that had originally been lent, could then be claimed by the then bearer, usually from one of the same banks listed on each interest coupon. They were anonymous; the name of the owner of each bond was never recorded. Only if a bank held a bond in safe custody for a customer, was the name of the current owner of the bond, ever recorded. Because of all this, Bearer Bonds were a good way to hide wealth, avoid taxation and facilitate illegal transfers and transactions. In the 21$^{st}$ century, they were to be largely abolished by numerous governments for these very reasons.

Edwards pondered on all this as he walked down Cheapside; as he arrived at Saint Paul's tube station he started to muse to himself. "I could go down those steps," he thought. "There is nothing to stop me taking a train to Heathrow Airport and, then, taking a flight to South America. I could choose a country that has no extradition treaty with the United Kingdom. There I could live like a King and would never need to work again."

He quickly dismissed all thought of this massive crime; he would never be able to live with himself, let alone with the fear of eventually being caught and being brought back to England for trial and a long prison sentence. "My word is my bond," thought Edwards wryly. That was the "working motto" of the City of London, where trust in a person was everything, and he intended to live by it. He entered the bank building where he was due to deposit the Bearer Bonds that he was carrying; this particular bank had just bought the bonds from Edwards's current employer.

# 4

After university, Edwards had joined a leading merchant bank. First, he had served in their International Banking Department, but then he had been given a series of special projects. The last of these had been to research and write a paper for the Board of Directors on the International Bond Market. The Eurobond Market, as it was also called, had been established in the City of London from the late 1960s, and it especially dealt in Bearer Bonds denominated in United States dollars.

The dollar had now replaced the British pound as the largest international currency, and issuing, selling and dealing in Eurobonds, especially those denominated in dollars, had become a big business. Edwards had been given a desk in a small room with three other men; one was a Viscount and one was rapidly losing his wife to a Royal Prince. After a quick divorce, she would marry her Prince and take a Royal title. The third man, who, like Edwards, had not attended a major public school, became his mentor and helped him with the production of his paper.

The reason for this research soon became clear; Edwards was seconded to a new, smaller bank that his employer had set up, in partnership, with a large American bank. They occupied the 14$^{th}$ floor of a just-completed, grey-blue glass, City skyscraper. The views from the windows were magnificent, but they were, at first, without any carpets or many of the other comforts normally associated with such a business. Edwards was supposed to put into practice what he had recently studied; he began to deal in Eurobonds, but he had no one else to work with or to help him with this activity. He had to deal with everything himself; that was the reason he was personally delivering this "High Value Packet" today.

Soon he grew tired of having total responsibility and the frustration of having few of the expected comforts or facilities. He decided to leave and found a new role at a leading stockbroking firm that appointed him as their Chief Analyst for the Eurobond market. He was now part of a small department within this larger organisation; just his Director, who was from Germany, a bond trader called Philip and his assistant. Edwards had the part-time use of two junior analysts, who also studied the share market, the main business of this stockbroker. They were there to help him write analytical papers and buy and sell recommendations for Eurobonds. These would then be distributed to the firm's many clients.

Edwards had been at his new firm about six months. One day, his Director called him over to his desk. His Director was fastidious, but progressive, and had joined the firm from a stockbroking company in Frankfurt. "We must all take on some marketing activity," said the Director. "I have decided that you will take on Italy and Ticino, the Italian-speaking part of Switzerland."

"But I speak no Italian," said Edwards.

"That does not matter. They all speak good English anyway," said his Director, who, of course, spoke perfect English.

So it was that Edwards was excited to find himself on a regular visit every two to three months. First a flight to Milan to stay for a few days there, a day visit by train to Turin to meet with one of the oldest banks in Italy, and then, on another train, to visit the Swiss city of Lugano where he would stay for a few more days. For him it was a revelation; he had already visited Paris, Luxembourg and Amsterdam with Philip, but now he had his own territory to visit, to market to, and there to try to develop new Eurobond business.

He enjoyed Milan; he always stayed at the luxurious Hotel Principe di Savoia on the Piazza della Repubblica. This was conveniently located near to most of the major banks he had to visit. Close by, too, was the magnificent Milan Cathedral; the largest Gothic building in Italy. Rebuilt over many years from 1386, when a disastrous fire had destroyed its predecessor on the same site, its architects had included Leonardo da Vinci. Edwards had also managed to visit Leonardo's masterpiece, "The Last Supper", in the Milan Convent of Santa Maria delle Grazie.

When Edwards wanted some amusement, he would walk to the Galleria Vittorio Emanuele ll, one of the oldest and probably the finest shopping arcades in the world. Opened in 1877 and named after the first king of a united Italy, its spectacular architecture of arching coloured glass and cast iron domes impressed him. He gazed at the overpriced merchandise in the shop windows but, most of all, he watched the people, particularly the beautiful, well-dressed women, who seemed to frequent it.

On each of his visits to Milan, he asked the hotel concierge to book him a ticket, which he always paid for himself. It was for an evening performance at the famous opera house, the Teatro Alla Scala. There he sat entranced at each superb performance, usually of an opera by Giuseppe Verdi, and was grateful for the opportunities that his newfound international life was bringing to him.

One of the banks he visited in Milan had been founded the previous century and, until its collapse in 1982, was considered to be a truly Catholic bank with its main shareholder being the Istituto per le Opere di Religione, usually known at the Vatican Bank. This Milan bank was the second largest privately owned bank in Italy and a major investment bank; as such, it was a prime potential client for Edwards's stockbroking firm and its Eurobond business. He got to know a number of its senior staff and was then asked to meet its General Manager.

Edwards remembered well the first time he had met this man; he was shown into a plush office on the top floor of the building. Behind the large desk sat a short, sallow man with a large moustache. He rose to introduce himself. His English was not very good, but Edwards managed to make clear what he wanted; to make the bank a major client of his firm. The man smiled at him; his face was illuminated by the desk lamp that was shining into it. Only then did Edwards realise what was wrong. It was a bright, sunny day outside, but the lights in this office were on. All the heavy curtains were drawn against the light coming in from the windows.

On his second meeting with this General Manager, he had treated the man with even greater respect. By then, Edwards had heard the stories about him. Throughout Italy, he was known as "God's Banker" and was considered to be very close to the American-born Archbishop who was the current Chairman of the Vatican Bank. The story was that this man controlled very large amounts of money sourced from the Vatican itself. By this time, Edwards had given the man his own nickname of "The Banker."

On this visit, he made a real effort to impress the man with his knowledge of the Eurobond market. Suddenly, the General Manager stopped him; he reached out and opened a drawer in his desk. From the drawer, he took out a small box. Then, from the small box, he took out a business card which he handed to Edwards. He smiled at Edwards. "This is my very good friend and colleague," he said. "You must visit him and explain what you do."

# 5

After every visit to Milan, Edwards then took the train, across the border, to the Swiss city of Lugano. He used to stay at least two nights there in a hotel that was clean and efficient but, by no means, as luxurious and elegant as that he had used in Milan. The Italian-speaking city of Lugano was full of banks. Some were international banks, the subsidiaries of American or British banks, or from many other countries around the world. Others were the branches of major Swiss banks or medium-sized or smaller Swiss private banks. There were also the Swiss subsidiaries of Italian banks.

Edwards had a very busy time; he used to sprint from one meeting to another, at the same time feverishly dictating notes, about his previous meeting, into a small recording machine which he had brought with him. He hardly had time to look at his beautiful surroundings; the city was set by the side of the clear, sparkling waters of Lake Lugano, and around it stood the often snow-capped peaks of the Italian Alps.

Edwards was usually amused during his train journey to this Swiss city. He left Milan Central Station in a first class coach; each compartment had six seats. Usually, to each side of him and opposite him, sat Italian businessmen in their smart suits. Above their heads, in the luggage racks, they had all carefully placed their bulging suitcases. The train rattled north; at first the land was flat, but soon the mountains appeared. On the border between Italy and Switzerland was the little town of Chiasso, where the train stopped for a border inspection. Here the Italian border guards entered the train, to inspect the passengers and their baggage; Edwards watched as beads of sweat broke out on the foreheads of his fellow passengers.

He knew well, by now, what was in their bulging suitcases. For years, Italy had suffered from the export of "flight capital"; the smuggling abroad of large amounts of Italian Lire banknotes, to be converted into other, stronger, currencies and deposited into foreign banks away from the Italian tax authorities. It amused him because, over the course of his next two days in Lugano, he knew that he would see one or two of his fellow passengers again. This time, they would be depositing large bundles of Italian Lire notes at the counters of the banks he was visiting!

But the Italian guards were not efficient; a quick glance into the compartment and they were gone. He never once saw them even ask for a passport or look into the case of a fellow passenger. "It was almost as if they had been ordered not to bother too much about the travellers on this train," Edwards thought. But this was Italy, and he was just beginning to understand that some things were never as they seemed. He remembered the story of the Italian Tax Inspector that he had been told; this official had a large desk. But the desk was placed the wrong way around, so that his "tax-paying" visitors could easily settle their total tax bill at a very low figure. To do this, they deposited a "brown envelope," full of banknotes, into one of the drawers of the desk, which had been so conveniently placed with its drawers facing towards them!

In his hotel room, in Lugano, Edwards took out the business card that "The Banker" had given him. It was in the name of Patrizio Andronotti, and he was the Manager of the branch of a large Swiss bank in Chiasso. The address of the bank and its telephone number were given on it. He decided to telephone him, the following day, and make an appointment to meet him. When he called, it proved easy; it was almost as if Andronotti was expecting his call. They agreed to meet the following morning; Edwards could easily break his journey by train back to Milan. He was not due to fly back to London from Milan until that evening.

# 6

Edwards had heard that the small town of Chiasso was a strange place. Built on the border, half of the town was in Switzerland and half was in Italy. Because petrol was cheap in Switzerland, there were a number of petrol stations on the Swiss side of the border, and Italian drivers used to cross the border to fill up the tanks of their cars. On the Swiss side, as well, there were branches of several Swiss banks and the Swiss branches of a number of Italian banks.

Along the border, there had been built, many years before, a number of houses; these houses were now famous. Many stories were told about how suitcases were seen to be carried into these houses, through their front doors, that were in Italy. Some of their cash contents, it was said, were then extracted inside the house as a fee. Then, the suitcases would be deposited, out of the back doors of the houses, which were in Switzerland, there to be collected by their Italian owners.

Edwards got off the train at Chiasso Station and walked down the main street; in the distance he could see the border crossing into Italy. Just a few buildings before the border, was located the bank that he was due to visit. He entered and asked to see Signor Andronotti. He was quickly shown into his office and accepted the inevitable offer of a good Italian coffee. Everything about Andronotti was sleek; he wore a smartly cut Italian suit, a matching shirt and tie and soft, handmade Italian shoes. His black hair was brushed back from his tanned face. He revealed perfect, white teeth as he smiled a welcome. His black eyes and aquiline nose completed the picture. He oozed so much charm that, straight away, Edwards did not like the man!

Edwards presented his business card and explained that Signor Andronotti's name had been mentioned by the General Manager of the particular bank in Milan that he visited regularly. Immediately, Andronotti confirmed that "This gentleman is a very good friend of mine." He went on to explain that he had met him many years before and had more recently started to look after some of his private affairs. "He wanted me to explain to you what I do and what my firm does," Edwards told him. He went into his usual "sales pitch" which was, by now, near perfect. Andronotti listened to him politely. When he had finished, Andronotti looked at him directly. "I think that we can do some business with you," he said. "I will contact you within the next seven days."

Edwards made his way back to the train station; he felt very pleased about how this short meeting had gone. It was, of course, one of many meetings that had taken place during this trip. When he was back in the office, he would have to transcribe his notes and the recordings he had made into a full Visit Report for his Director and his colleagues. He would certainly include this meeting in his notes and was hopeful that maybe Andronotti would keep his word and, actually, do some business with his firm. Maybe he was not such a "bad chap" after all; first impressions can sometimes be deceptive!

Back in his small department in London, Edwards carefully transcribed his notes and recordings. When this was finished, he had them typed out by the secretary who was attached to their section. He then personally distributed the typed Visit Report to his Director and his colleagues. The next day, his Director wanted to discuss his recent visit; the sharp-eyed German had spotted his visit to Chiasso. "How did this come about?" he asked. Edwards explained that it had been on the introduction of the General Manager of the Milan bank. The Director looked at him rather strangely. "We shall see what will happen," he said. "Either nothing will happen, or it could turn into something that will be very interesting."

# 7

A few days later, Edwards's telephone rang; it was Signor Andronotti calling him from Chiasso. After a polite exchange enquiring about their mutual health, Andronotti said, "I have decided that I would like to use you to buy some Bearer Bonds on behalf of a client." Edwards explained to him that he was only the bond analyst, who made contact to introduce his firm's investment ideas to prospective clients. He would have to pass him over now to their Senior Dealer to execute any transactions. He introduced Philip, on the telephone, and then let Philip get on with the actual business. "I am sure that Philip will be able to help you with fully up-to-date prices," he told

Andronotti. "He can make the purchases for you and then arrange for the delivery of your bonds."

Later that day, Edwards asked Philip how his conversation with Andronotti had gone? "Great," answered Philip. "I sold him twenty million dollars of various Bearer Bonds, mainly governments, at the best prices!" Edwards was surprised; he had never heard of a first deal from a new client of that size before.

Over the next two months, Andronotti called Philip every week or so and made more purchases in similar amounts. Edwards was at first delighted, but then became increasingly concerned about the growing cumulative size of the transactions. Just where was Andronotti getting this amount of investment funds from? After all, he was only a manager in an unimportant branch of a Swiss bank in a small town on the Italian border. He asked Philip about the size and regularity of the purchases.

"I think that it's ok," said Philip; his anticipated bonus was increasing every time he made a sale!

"But where is he getting the bonds delivered?" asked Edwards.

He has asked for all of them to be sent to the address of a lawyer in Liechtenstein," replied Philip.

The Principality of Liechtenstein is a small, land-locked, German-speaking, independent state sandwiched between Switzerland and Austria. Its history is bound up with the fortunes of the Liechtenstein family from Austria who, over the centuries, acquired large areas of land in Central Europe. The family name came from their castle in Austria. Karl the First of Liechtenstein, was made a Prince by the Holy Roman Emperor in the early 17th century and then acquired the land on which the modern state of Liechtenstein now stands. In

1719, Liechtenstein became a sovereign member state of the Holy Roman Empire and has remained independent ever since. The Napoleonic Wars brought many changes in Europe, and the Liechtenstein family sold most of their land and moved to live in their castle in Liechtenstein.

Edwards did his research and found out that Liechtenstein had a monetary union with Switzerland and used the Swiss Franc as its currency. It had one of the highest incomes per head in the world. Lacking any industry and resources, it had concentrated on the financial sector and had one of the lowest rates of personal and company taxation in Europe. Through the establishment of "Foundation" or "Trusts", lawyers and local banks in Liechtenstein could set up secret holdings of wealth and investments, of all kinds. These were for people who had the money and who could buy the best advice to escape from the scrutiny of their own government and their tax authorities. Edwards was now very worried, and he spoke to his Director about the situation. "Let us see how the position develops," was his laconic reply.

Edwards always had to read, among many other publications, the daily *Financial Times* newspaper. The "Pink One", as it is known in the City, is probably the best source, along with *The Wall Street Journal*, of financial intelligence in the world. A few days later, he was scouring the pages of the "FT" when an item caught his eye. "The Banker" had been promoted from General Manager to Chairman of his Milan-based bank. Edwards was relieved; surely this promotion showed that "The Banker" had done nothing wrong and that the actions that Edwards's firm was taking, presumably on his behalf, through the bank in Chiasso, had the full approval of the bank's shareholders.

He pointed out the article to his Director. The business relationship with Signor Andronotti continued; every other week or so, purchases of more Bearer Bonds, in similar amounts, were made by him. All the bonds were then sent, by secure transport, to the lawyer in Liechtenstein. The total amount he had purchased so far was now reaching nearly two hundred million United States dollars!

One day, in a quiet period, Philip was reading that day's " FT", when he let out a low whistle. "Our client has just been arrested!" he said. There it was, in black and white; Patrizio Andronotti and a junior colleague had been arrested by the Swiss Police. Over subsequent days, more newspaper reports appeared. They had both been charged with illegally issuing guarantees in the name of their Head Office in Zurich to Italian investors. Their Head Office knew nothing about these transactions. The money deposited had then been "laundered" through Liechtenstein and sometimes, some of the money had even been returned to Italy, to be invested by these two bank officials in certain projects, for their own benefit.

The total amount involved in this fraud was reported at some five hundred million United States dollars, but the two bank officials were also suspected of other illegal financial activities that could not be proved. Their trial followed quickly, and they pleaded guilty. Both were sentenced to just seven years each in a comfortable Swiss prison.

For Edwards, this news came as a great shock. He could not believe that the charming Patrizio Andronotti had been capable of such a massive fraud! He fully expected that he personally, or his firm, would be called to give evidence against Andronotti or, at least, to take part in investigations to bring further charges against him. He rehearsed carefully, in his head, what he would say as evidence, if he was called upon to do so. But time went by and Edwards's firm was never contacted; it was almost as if the Swiss authorities were embarrassed about what these two men had done and that they did not want to risk raising further, the profile of their crimes, by making any international enquiries.

# 8

Christmas was approaching and things were not looking good for the year-end bonuses. As well as the loss of Signor Andronotti as an important client, prices on the bond market, generally, had turned down and the volume of daily business had substantially declined. Life in the office was boring: there was little work to do in the department. Edwards, Philip and his assistant took to playing cards and other games, while their Director fretted about how some additional business could be brought in. The team became more and more disillusioned and even started playing tricks on each other, to while away their time in the office. One morning, Philip asked Edwards if he was free for lunch that day?

"Yes, I am free," replied Edwards.

"I have invited two guys out for a good lunch before Christmas," said Philip. "We will meet them at the restaurant at twelve o'clock."

The lunch was held at one of the best and most expensive restaurants in the City where Philip had booked a table. When they met up with their two guests, Edwards recognised them immediately. They were two Fund Managers, working for a British government-owned organisation that handled investment funds belonging to both the British government and other overseas governments. He knew that Philip had made a real effort to get to know them. They sat down at their table and Philip ordered, for everyone, their choice of aperitifs.

"Let me order some Beluga caviar," said Philip. The order was made, and then Philip called over the Wine Waiter. "There is only one thing to drink with that," he said to their two guests. "Neat, ice-cold vodka." The caviar was brought, together with a chilled bottle of the best Russian vodka, with four small glasses, that also had been chilled to help keep cold the ample supply of the drink.

The fine meal proceeded; after the caviar, a selection of the finest Italian antipasto was served with an expensive Italian white wine, carefully selected by Philip. "What is good today for the main course?" Philip asked the Head Waiter. "I can recommend the pheasant, sir," was the answer. Everybody agreed with that choice; when it arrived, Edwards was surprised. He had expected just some slices of meat; instead, each diner was presented with his own whole pheasant! This was complemented by the finest vegetables and several bottles of a grand, Claret wine, selected carefully, for its high cost, by Philip.

Their guests grew more and more animated and friendly. When the time came for dessert, Philip checked whether his idea, was acceptable to all of them. He then ordered Crepes Suzette for the table. They were surrounded by waiters; a small spirit stove was brought and the crepes were flambéed with Grand Marnier liqueur, in front of them.

"Would you like some cheese now?" asked Philip, once their dessert course had been completed. But everybody agreed that they had already eaten too much. "Then some coffee and liqueurs," ordered Philip. "And of course, bring the cigar box as well." It was not until after four o'clock that their guests indicated that they had better leave and try and put in an appearance back at their office. Warm goodbyes were said, and only after their guests had left, did Philip call for the bill.

"Make sure you put something on for your excellent service," said Philip to the waiter and paid using the American Express Gold Card issued to him by their firm.

"However much was that?" asked Edwards, now getting rather worried about the cost.

"Well over five hundred Pounds," replied Philip mischievously. "I wish that I could have made it more," he added.

"But however are you going to justify that cost?" asked Edwards.

"You will see," was all that Philip would say.

By the next morning, Edwards had just about recovered from the lunch. After the enormous meal and all the alcoholic drinks, he and Philip had staggered back to the office, collected their things and gone home. Edwards had woken that morning from a deep sleep with a bad headache, but a couple of Aspirin tablets, had soon settled that.

As he had participated in this very expensive entertainment, the previous day, Edwards was still worried about how Philip could ever justify the high expenditure. At about eleven o'clock, Philip's telephone started ringing; he was on the line for the rest of the morning. His assistant was very busy checking prices. Edwards could not hear what was going on. As lunchtime approached, he asked Philip how his morning had gone?

Excellent!" said Philip. "Our friends from yesterday have just been placing some business with me; some sales but mostly buy orders in large amounts. So far, I have made a profit of over five hundred thousand Pounds for the firm, and I think that there is more to come! All this adds to my bonus at the end of this year!"

# 9

Christmas came and then the New Year celebrations. Edwards was not yet married and, not having much to do in London, he left for a quiet holiday with his parents in the genteel, seaside, holiday resort in South Devon, that they had made their home. On his return to the office, there were high hopes for a renewed level of business in the new year but they were not fulfilled. The Eurobond market was stagnant, and there was very little activity by which the department could make any money. Edwards's trips to Italy and Switzerland were cancelled to save costs, and Edwards began to fear that, if things did not improve quickly, his firm would be unable to pay his salary and he would be made redundant. He confessed his views to Philip, who had become his confidant. "I am beginning to look around, too, for a new job," was Philip's response.

Fortunately for Edwards, a friend from his university days, had mentioned that the merchant bank that he had joined was looking for more staff and he suggested that he could arrange for Edwards to meet the Senior Director of their Banking Department. Edwards went, one afternoon, for what turned out to be an informal interview and was offered a position at this prestigious bank. He was very relieved to have this opportunity to change his job and found himself at a desk in a large, open-plan room. He soon realised, once again, that he was in a minority. Of the people working there, he was the only one who had not attended a top-class public school.

Rather incongruously with his new surroundings, Edwards still met up with Philip for lunch. Philip was a real East End "barrow boy", but had immense charm and a great sense of humour. Edwards was always reminded of the story of how Philip had met his wife. He had been speeding in the expensive sports car, that the firm gave him as part of his salary package, when he had collided with a lamp post. His future wife was walking past at the time, and seriously admonished him for his stupidity. Philip had invited her out and they were soon married!

At one of their lunches, Philip announced that he and his wife were moving to New York; he had been offered an exceptionally well-paid position at a stockbroking firm in the Wall Street financial district of the city. Edwards was delighted for him and kept in touch, even after he had moved there. Soon Edwards himself was married and, on their first overseas holiday, he took his new wife to visit America.

They were invited to stay with Philip and his wife in their plush New Jersey apartment. Edwards remembered the fabulous view from the balcony at night; the lights of downtown New York were just spectacular. Each morning, Philip drove them over the George Washington Bridge, and left them in downtown Manhattan, to wander around in their own time and see the sights of this great city. They then went back to his office in late afternoon, for him to run them back to their apartment. One evening, Philip surprised them with a trip to a restaurant he knew in Harlem. He carefully deposited them at the restaurant door, before finding somewhere safe to park his car. They were given a window table; half-way through his meal, Edwards looked up. There were three hungry-looking, black faces pressed against the window watching them eat!

Back in London, the years seem to speed by. Edwards had now left banking; he had become generally disillusioned with the world of the City with its drive for continuous quick profits, greed, personal bonuses and its "dog-eat-dog" attitudes. Instead, he had moved over to working in what he considered to be "the real world." He had become an adviser on all things financial to a major, international group of contracting and engineering companies.

He still read his daily copy of the *Financial Times* to keep up with the international financial news. One morning he spotted an unusual item. A Eurobond dealer, working for a major Swiss bank in Zurich, had, the previous morning, arrived at his office as usual. He had sat down at his desk. Then he had pulled a small automatic pistol out from his pocket and shot himself dead, through the head!

Soon, speculative articles began to appear that he was part of a conspiracy working with others to defraud his bank. A few days later, a short announcement appeared; Philip had been dismissed from his Wall Street firm, and an investigation had been started into illegal transactions that he had been carrying out with the dead Swiss dealer. Philip returned home in disgrace; nobody would now employ him.

A few months later, Philip took a flight to Geneva, where he was immediately arrested and charged by the Swiss authorities. Some eight million United States dollars were missing from the Swiss bank, and this amount was believed to have been shared between Philip and the dead man. A guilty plea ensured that Philip was sentenced to only five years, in a comfortable Swiss jail!

# 10

At seven-thirty in the morning of the tenth of June 1982, a postal clerk, crossing Blackfriars Bridge, over the River Thames, in London, noticed a body, hanging by the neck, from a rope attached to some scaffolding surrounding part of the bridge. The City of London Police were called and, together with a patrol boat of the Thames Division of the Metropolitan Police, they managed to recover the corpse. It was the body of a well-nourished, middle-aged man. He was wearing an expensive suit and black shoes. Inside the pockets of his suit were stuffed some bricks and around fifteen thousand United States dollars, denominated in various currencies.

The body was subsequently identified as belonging to Roberto Calvi, who, until he had been dismissed, the previous day, had been the Chairman of Banco Ambrosiano in Milan. The previous day, also, his Private Secretary had, apparently, committed suicide, by jumping to her death from the fifth floor of the Banco Ambrosiano building.

Roberto Calvi had been widely known in Italy as "God's Banker" because of his close relationship with the Vatican and with the American Archbishop Paul Marcinkus, who had run the Vatican Bank for some eighteen years. Only five days before his death, Calvi had written directly to Pope John Paul ll, warning that a collapse of Banco Ambrosiano, would result in a "catastrophe of unimaginable proportions" for the Catholic Church.

Just two weeks after this letter, Banco Ambrosiano had indeed collapsed, and an amount estimated to be up to one and a half billion United States dollars was discovered to be missing. It was eventually determined, that much of this money had been siphoned off, from the Vatican Bank, the main shareholder in Banco Ambrosiano. Nevertheless, in 1984, the Vatican Bank agreed to pay out two hundred and twenty-four million United Stated dollars to some of the creditors of Banco Ambrosiano, in recognition of the "moral involvement" of the Vatican Bank in the Milan bank's collapse.

Edwards was fascinated by this continuing story, and consumed every piece of news and every article that he could find about this affair. He remembered well the man, whom he had nicknamed "The Banker", and now he had begun to understand the mystery that had always somehow surrounded him. Edwards also now finally understood why the man's office curtains were always closed. Sitting behind his desk, he would have presented a perfect target for a sniper's bullet!

But Roberto Calvi had been well protected; he had been a member of the secret and illegal Masonic Lodge in Rome known as Propaganda Due. Founded in 1945, its Masonic Charter was withdrawn in 1976; by that time, it was an ultra-right-wing organisation, a "state within a state." Its members included prominent journalists, politicians, industrialists and military leaders. It also included the heads of all three Italian intelligence services. The Lodge symbol was the "Black Friar", and this soon inspired the rumour that, Calvi's death, hanging under Blackfriars Bridge, was a warning to other Lodge members, never to talk about the secret discussions that had taken place within the Lodge.

In 1978, the Italian Central Bank, the Bank of Italy, had produced a report on Banco Ambrosiano which found that billions of Italian Lire had been exported illegally from Italy, by various means, from this bank. This led to criminal investigations, and Roberto Calvi, by then the bank's Chairman, was arrested. He was tried for illegally transferring the equivalent of only twenty-seven million United States dollars out of Italy. He was found guilty and sentenced to a four year suspended prison sentence and fined nearly twenty million United States dollars.

He was released on bail pending an appeal, but, he would never lose his position as Chairman of Banco Ambrosiano, until the Bank of Italy stripped him of that position, the very day before his death. Rumours of large amounts of money, belonging to the Cosa Nostra, otherwise known as the Mafia, being exported abroad through the "money laundering" mechanism of the Banco Ambrosiano and the Vatican Bank, were now rampant, but they were never proved. All the way through, Calvi's family maintained that he was an innocent man used and manipulated by other more powerful individuals.

# 11

Calvi's body appears never to have been properly examined. The first Coroner's Inquest, held in London, the month after his death, concluded that "The Banker" had committed suicide. The Calvi family maintained that his death had been a murder and used the services of an eminent barrister, to secure a second inquest. This happened one year later, and arrived at an "open verdict", indicating that the Court had been unable to determine the exact cause of death. Edwards followed the story avidly; it had been obvious to him straight away, given Calvi's background, that he had been murdered.

Eight days before his death, Roberto Calvi had disappeared from his Rome apartment, after shaving off his moustache. Using a passport in a false name, he had flown from Venice, via Zurich, to London. On the evening of the ninth of June 1982, a witness had seen two smartly dressed men collecting him from the flat in Chelsea where he had been staying. He was never seen alive again, and the two men were never traced. Edwards thought that it was almost as if the City of London Police and the City authorities were unable to admit that a Mafia murder could ever take place with impunity in the "Square Mile" of the City of London. They did not want their leading financial centre ever to be sullied with a "contract killing!"

It was not until 1991 that, out of frustration, the Calvi family asked a New York private investigation firm to properly examine the real circumstances of Roberto Calvi's death. As part of this two-year investigation, that the Calvi family commissioned, proper forensic tests were carried out for the first time by former Home Office scientists. They found that Calvi could not have hanged himself because of the lack of paint, dust and rust on his shoes, which proved that he could not have climbed over the scaffolding which surrounded that part of Blackfriars Bridge at the time of his death. These findings were immediately rejected out-of-hand by the British Home Office and the City of London Police.

Over the next six years, various former Mafia members, now turned informers, admitted that Calvi had been killed by their former organisation and even named those who had killed him. In 1998, an Italian Court, at last, ordered the exhumation of Roberto Calvi's body and commissioned a German forensic scientist to repeat the work carried out in 1991.

The report on this further forensic work was not published until October 2002; it completely confirmed the results of the report ten years earlier by the American investigation company. Furthermore, it concluded that the injuries to Calvi's neck were inconsistent with a normal suicide by hanging and that he had never touched the bricks found in his pockets. The German report stated that, with the high tide at the time of Calvi's death, the place on the scaffolding where the rope had been tied to hang him, could have been reached by a person standing in a boat. This had also been the conclusion of a second, secret report that the American firm of investigators had made to the Calvi family, ten years earlier.

In July 2003, Italian prosecutors concluded that the Mafia had killed Calvi, so that he could never blackmail former members of the "P2" Masonic Lodge or the Vatican and its Bank. They confirmed that he had been involved with handling substantial sums of money from the Mafia, some of which had probably been lost or stolen.

In September 2003, the City of London Police, at last, reopened their investigations into the death of Roberto Calvi, twenty-one years earlier, as a murder inquiry. For five years, from 2005, various individuals, including Licio Gelli, the Grand Master of the Propaganda Due Lodge, appeared before the Italian Courts charged, in one way or another, with a connection to Calvi's murder. But the evidence, by then, was insufficient, and they were all acquitted.

For Edwards, the face of "The Banker", framed in the light from the lamp on his desk, remained a vivid memory. So, too, did his enjoyable visits to Italy and Switzerland to market and sell the instruments of the Eurobond market that also could, so easily, provide the secrecy and easy transferability to promote fraud, theft and deception. As he had personally seen, the bearer form of these financial instruments, could lead some people astray and end in their disgrace and imprisonment. Sometimes, even, it could lead to their early and violent deaths!

THE END

# Whispers

-

*"Russia is a riddle, wrapped in a mystery, inside an enigma."*

— **Winston S. Churchill**

# 1

The plump, little man sat at the table. The light from the many ornate chandeliers, hanging from the ceiling, were reflected off his nearly bald head. Opposite him sat a well-dressed and well-coiffured lady; her steely, blue eyes were watching him very closely. He was dressed in a simple dark business suit with a white shirt and sombre tie. As she had been advised to do, she kept her eyes away from the strange birthmark on the top of his head. She had been told that he was very conscious of this defect. The luxurious, ornate room in which they were sitting glistened with gold leaf and many precious pictures. The room was within a huge and ancient fortress, to which she had been driven in convoy that morning. The fortress was in the middle of the capital city of this vast country.

Appearances are often very deceptive. The plump, little man controlled the fate of millions of his countrymen and women. At his command, thousands of intercontinental ballistic missiles could be unleashed, each tipped with a very powerful nuclear warhead. He was the Supreme Leader of his country. On both sides of him sat his advisers; his most trusted adviser and Private Secretary sat next to him on his right-hand side. On the opposite side of the table, the lady was flanked by her own advisers. On both sides of the table, there were carefully constructed piles of papers in front of each participant, and in the middle, there was every kind of refreshment available.

It had been a very long day of intense discussions, lengthened by the need for the overworked interpreters to translate carefully every word that was spoken. Both the Supreme Leader and the lady were experienced enough to pause, after every sentence they spoke, to allow the interpreters to catch up. This made true communication difficult, and the lady had to watch carefully for the Leader's gestures and facial expressions as he spoke, but then keep these intimate signals in mind, for when the translation of what he had said, arrived in her ears.

This was the last day of discussions; that evening a State Banquet would be held. Both leaders realised that they first had to refresh themselves, change and even have a few minutes of rest, so as to be in top form for this event. Substantial progress had been achieved in the discussions over the last two days. But some valid conclusions still needed to be written up by their advisers overnight and signed by both leaders, before the lady flew home the following morning. The atmosphere was tense, because neither side wanted to lose momentum, but both also realised that there was little time left.

The little man was a consummate negotiator; he would not have reached his position if he were not. He wanted, at this meeting, to leave certain issues in the air, without a final decision. He wanted to give this lady sufficient for her to feel that her visit had been a success, but then leave it to her initiative to make the next move later on in the year. Diplomacy is like a game of tennis, he thought. You returned the ball for a while, just to see what your opponent would do. He still enjoyed the occasional tennis game, particularly with his Private Secretary, who sat to his right. Theirs was a very long friendship; it went back to their primary school days in a small, provincial town, miles away from the capital city of this immense country, which he now governed.

He decided to bring the discussions to an end; he smiled at the lady and indicated that they should both now take a little time off to prepare for the dinner that evening. She, of course, had to agree, as he had left her no other option. Papers were shuffled on both sides of the table, ready to be packed away in locked briefcases. The little man had decided what his next move would be, once the lady had somehow signalled her intent. He turned to his Private Secretary, inclined his head and whispered something into his ear. The man did not hear clearly what was said, and the Supreme Leader had to repeat it in a louder tone. He was confident that nobody else in the room would understand what he had just said, but that his life-long friend and colleague would understand what he now had to prepare for.

Across the table, one of the lady's aides caught sight of this movement and instantly inclined his head towards the pair opposite. Behind his left ear was a hearing aid joined by a wire to an earpiece; any ordinary observer would have thought him slightly deaf. But the Supreme Leader had been advised, by his own intelligence service, that this was not a hearing aid. It was a powerful microphone tuned in to hear every sound in the direction that this man turned his head. In his pocket, he had also been told, connected to this microphone, the man carried a state-of-the-art recording device. Although this man held the diplomatic post of the Second Secretary at their Embassy, the Supreme Leader knew that he was actually a member of the Secret Intelligence Service of the lady's country.

The spy was watching them carefully; he had been trained in the interpretation of body language. The Leader's Private Secretary had stiffened imperceptibly and nodded slightly; the spy knew instinctively that what had been whispered by the Supreme Leader was not a joke or a comment. It had been a command!

# 2

The lady sat back in the comfortable back seat of the expensive car ; on her side on the front wing of the car, her nation's flag fluttered proudly. Her Private Secretary sat beside her but knew, through long experience, that he should only speak if he was spoken to. The car was in a convoy of other vehicles accompanied by a large police escort. They drove down the special middle lane given over to official vehicles, so that they were not bothered by any normal traffic or the ordinary citizens of this capital city. Her car soon swept through the gates and up the drive to her Embassy. She was escorted up the steps and through the front door. Her Ambassador, who had been at the discussions with her, soon arrived in one of the following vehicles.

As soon as they were both safely inside and sitting within a room that had been "swept" to identify any form of electronic surveillance, she turned to him. She fixed him with her piercing, blue eyes and asked, "What did you think of today?" A lesser man would have found it difficult to answer such a direct question from this particular lady, but the Ambassador had many years of experience in the Diplomatic Service and indeed had been Ambassador here for sufficient time to know this country and its leadership well.

He was also well aware that they were still not one hundred per cent secure; he had been briefed by experts that this country had developed very powerful directional microphone technology which could, even at a distance, pick up conversations taking place within a room from the vibrations generated in the glass of the windows. This room looked out onto the front gardens of the Embassy, and he was conscious that they might still be overheard.

He smiled at the lady who he knew could still be susceptible to male charm. "It is difficult to say, Prime Minister," he said quietly. "I think that we should consider this at our Morning Meeting." The Prime Minister nodded; she had taken the hint that the Morning Meeting would be held in the carefully constructed interior room of the

Embassy, made especially for such secure meetings. Within this room was another room, the walls of which were of special glass impregnated with a fine wire mesh. It was a so-called "Faraday Cage" that carefully shielded those inside against electromagnetic waves and any known form of advanced electronic surveillance.

For security reasons, the Prime Minister was staying at the Embassy and so was her Private Secretary, who had to be on hand every minute of the day and night. Other members of the British Delegation were not so lucky; they had been placed in a luxury hotel but, prior to boarding the aircraft to fly to Moscow, they had been severely warned of the dangers that might await them. Total surveillance of their every move and word was expected; hidden microphones and cameras would be everywhere. They were warned not to parade naked around their hotel room, but to always have a towel around them and even to change under the bedclothes, if possible, to avoid compromising photographs.

The more obvious risks of "Honey Traps" were explained; handsome young women or men, making themselves available for sexual activity, were to be avoided at all costs. The excessive consumption of alcohol, which could lead to "loose tongues," even when speaking to colleagues inside certain known secure locations, must also be avoided. It was now the second half of the 1980's and for over forty years, the world had been divided between the Communist "East" and the Capitalist "West." The "Cold War" had developed between the two sides, and once in Russia, the British delegation could expect total and constant hidden surveillance.

The Prime Minister had no such difficulties; she decided on a short rest and then a long bath before changing into the gown that she had already chosen for the State Banquet that evening. Her official car, accompanied by the other vehicles and the police escort, swept her back to the Kremlin for dinner. It was a glittering occasion in the huge ballroom of the Grand Kremlin Palace. This was just one of the five palaces and four cathedrals that stood within the Kremlin Wall, topped by its towers, that surrounded this huge and ancient complex.

Inside, standing alongside her host, the Prime Minister was introduced to a long line of other guests, who queued up to meet them. Although the numerous male ministers and leading citizens, she was introduced to, all wore sombre dark suits and ties, their wives were not bound by such conventions. Fashionable dresses, no doubt bought during long and expensive shopping visits to London or Paris, abounded. The large amounts of jewellery that they all wore would have been quite at home in the Kremlin during the time of the Tsars.

Seated to her left, her host, Mikhail Sergeyevich Gorbachev, General Secretary of the Communist Party of the Union of Soviet Socialist Republics, was charming. His command of English, for a leader of the Soviet Union, was remarkable. Just in case, an interpreter sat between them, well back out of the limelight. But her services were not needed during the whole evening. The food had been specially selected to please their British guests, and the fine French wines complemented the food perfectly.

The meal over, the General Secretary stood up to speak. He spoke in good English. In Russian fashion, there were first numerous toasts that he had to propose, including one to the health of the Queen. He then welcomed the Prime Minister and her delegation in the spirit of friendship and the wish to further good relations between her country and the Soviet Union. The British Prime Minister, Margaret Thatcher, replied in the same manner, reading from a carefully prepared speech that had been through many drafts, mainly between her Private Secretary, the Foreign Office and the British Ambassador in Moscow. At the end of her speech, she remained standing to toast the health of their hosts and the future friendship between Britain and the Soviet Union.

The next morning, at precisely eight o'clock, participants in the Morning Meeting assembled in the most secure room of the Embassy. The door was locked, but, even within the "Faraday Cage," those present still spoke to each other in low tones, almost in whispers. The Prime Minister took the lead, asking all those there for their views on the progress that had been made, over the previous two days of discussions. The British Ambassador led off with his view of the previous day's proceedings, based upon his years of experience of dealing with Russia. He was followed by the most senior Foreign Office man from London present, and then comments were heard from the more junior officials. The Prime Minister's piercing blue eyes swept around the table. "Are we to conclude, gentlemen," she said sternly, "that we can come to no specific conclusions about the last two days of discussions?"

The more junior officials assumed the pose of rabbits caught in a car's headlights; they felt that they were back at school and that the Head Mistress was annoyed with them. The Ambassador came to their rescue.

"I think that it is very difficult, Prime Minister, to read a man like the General Secretary," he said. "We must go away and carefully analyse the proceedings of the last two days."

His Second Secretary, who had, up to then, remained silent, suddenly interjected. "There is something!" he said. "My microphone picked up a strange remark that he made to his Private Secretary. It seemed to be important and he was ordering him to do something. But, although I speak Russian, I cannot understand it. I played it back to myself several times last night, but it did not help. It really needs some Russian language experts to listen to it again and again."

The Prime Minister rose from her chair and so did everyone else in the room. "I assume that we are due at the Kremlin to sign the Joint Communique at ten o'clock, as arranged," she said. "I would like to read the text you have agreed with the other side in my car, please." Then she turned to her Private Secretary. "Make sure my bags are in the car. We go straight from the signing to the airport."

# 3

Edwards was watching his colleague very carefully. Desmond was fussing around with cream and sugar for the large cup of coffee that he was about to pass to Edwards. He was, as always, very smartly dressed. Edwards liked this man's style; he was always consistent, suave and confident. Edwards had had a difficult drive in to the office that morning; the traffic had been terrible. He had a top-of-the-range company car, free petrol and a parking space. He was taxed a nominal sum on these items but, although it added driving time to his working day, this method of travel was preferable to being crushed with other commuters on crowded and unreliable public transport.

Edwards had been in this company for over five years now; he had joined from working for a prestigious merchant bank in the City of London. He was now the adviser on all things financial to a major group of construction companies and worked from an office block in West London. The activities of this group covered the world and Edwards had always to be fully aware of what was happening in a multitude of countries.

The summons to meet Desmond had come early that morning from Desmond's Personal Assistant. It was always a pleasure for Edwards to meet Desmond. Along with the man's charm, you were always served an excellent coffee in a proper cup and saucer. Desmond kept a special coffee machine by his PA's desk and always offered his visitors a freshly ground cup. "Better than the instant coffee in a mug that I am used to," thought Edwards, as he watched the man.

He thought back to what he knew about Desmond; his biography had been distributed to senior staff when he had joined the firm some five months ago. Desmond had joined from another construction group as a Marketing Director, but, Edwards had noticed that, after graduating in Modern Languages from a top university, there seemed to be strange gaps in the man's career. It was office rumour that he was paid an exceptionally high salary and had some excellent contacts.

In their previous meetings, they had got to know each other quite well. Desmond did not drive in to the office; he had a pied-a-terre in London and had a short, easy Tube journey, to the office, every morning. At the weekends, he returned to his wife and three daughters at his home in the Chilterns. He had joked, with Edwards that, "At the weekends, I have no male company, except for my dog!" He had mentioned that his father had served as an officer in the Special Operations Executive during the Second World War. The SOE was the highly secret organisation, that had been set up by Churchill, to promote espionage, sabotage and special reconnaissance behind enemy lines in the parts of Europe that had been invaded by the Nazis.

The previous year, Edwards had been invited to lunch at the Special Forces Club; a discreet building in a side street in Knightsbridge, located somewhere behind Harrods. His host had been the most senior and prestigious member of this Club. In front of the solid black door, Edwards had pressed the button on the intercom and announced his name and who he was meeting. He was conscious that he was being scrutinised by several CCTV cameras attached above the door. The lock on the door buzzed open and he pushed his way in. Given the name of his host, he was immediately treated with great deference. His coat was taken and he was directed up the staircase, lined with photographs, to the Bar where his host was waiting.

The Bar and the Dining Room were rather Spartan, when compared with other London Clubs that Edwards had visited. His host was a tall, lank Scotsman of great charm; after a lunch of typical "Club" food, but complemented by a good bottle of wine, his host had shown him out. As they descended the staircase, he had pointed out the numerous photographs to Edwards. "All members of the SOE," he had said. Edwards looked carefully; they were all young and a good number of them were pretty women.

"But so many of them were girls," said Edwards.

"Churchill used them because they would not raise suspicion in the minds of the Germans," replied his host.

At last, Desmond had sat down; they chatted together about a few of the construction projects that Desmond was working on in a number of countries. Desmond asked Edwards his opinion on the possibility of raising finance to build them. "Without the money, nothing will happen," he observed. Edwards agreed with that statement wholeheartedly. Too many members of the Marketing Department seemed, to Edwards, to live on another planet. They, too often, brought him "wild dreams" about projects that had not been properly costed and, that, it would be impossible, in any case, to finance.

Edwards replied to Desmond's questions, about the possibilities of finding finance for his projects, as accurately and concisely, as he could.

Suddenly, Desmond changed the subject and looked Edwards directly in the eye. "Is it correct that your wife speaks Russian?" he politely asked.

# 4

Edwards was not put out by this question. By now, he was very experienced in the international business world; he had travelled extensively and had met people of many different types and nationalities. "Yes, she does," he replied. "She studied it at school and then took a degree in Russian Language and Literature at the University of London." Desmond appeared interested. Edwards was very proud of his wife's achievements. "She has acted as a translator and as an official interpreter at a number of conferences," he added. "Last year, she even attended the meeting of the International Dostoevsky Society. It was held in a castle on an island in the middle of a lake in the Austrian Salzkammergut."

Desmond looked at him; he lowered his voice. "Would she do me a favour?" he asked. "Some of my friends have been trying to understand a particular Russian phrase. I speak reasonable Russian, but I cannot understand it and neither can they. If I write it down, will you take it to her and see if she can translate it, please?"

Edwards had readily agreed; "I am sure that my wife would not mind," he had said. Desmond had taken out a small piece of paper from his wallet and then carefully copied down the phrase on the top page of an office pad. He tore off the sheet of paper and handed it to

Edwards. Edwards looked at it carefully; it meant nothing to him. But he was surprised that Desmond had not written it out in the Cyrillic alphabet, used by the Russians, which his wife knew well. Instead, Desmond had written the phrase out phonetically, as it would sound to a listener. Desmond thanked him for his help and asked him to please pass on his compliments to his wife. Then, they both returned to the rest of their busy day.

Driving home that evening, with the piece of paper in his pocket, Edwards thought of what had happened as a result of his lunch at the Special Forces Club. Soon after that, he had lunched with his host again. This time, they had met at another of the Clubs where his host was a member. This one was in Pall Mall and was one of the plusher, more traditional Gentlemen's Clubs in London which carefully guarded who would be admitted as a member. As always, his host was full of charm. It was difficult to remember, that it was rumoured, that he had personally killed over forty men with his bare hands! After an excellent lunch, they retired to the Club's "Smoking Room," where, over coffee, brandy and cigars, his host had turned to him.

Lowering his voice, Colonel David Stirling had asked Edwards, whether he was prepared to meet "one of his people" and go on a "little trip" as a favour to him? Edwards was flattered; he had been introduced to David Stirling by his Managing Director, another charming Scotsman, who had, some years before, recruited Edwards to his present employment.

Edwards had quickly found out about David Stirling's background. David, before the Second World War, had been a mountaineer, then, as an Army officer in the war, had founded an elite unit to carry out reconnaissance and sabotage behind German lines in North Africa. The unit was given the deliberately misleading name of "L

Detachment, Special Air Service Brigade." After the first, badly judged raid, which had caused British loss of life, the unit succeeded in showing its worth by destroying numerous German aircraft and facilities. The unit, eventually, became established as the Special Air Service, the precursor to all such Special Forces which, as a new military concept, was taken up by other governments throughout the world.

David Stirling was to be knighted in 1990, just before he died at the age of 75, having, as he had told Edwards, secretly advised the Prime Minister on the security of certain critical aspects of Britain's infrastructure. David Stirling was a very impressive man with connections to all the right places; after a visit to Washington, he had confided to Edwards that he had been invited to the White House to meet President Ronald Reagan. Edwards had next met David at his offices in South Audley Street from where he ran, with several associates, a private company providing weapons and military support to other friendly countries.

There David had introduced Edwards to Brian, a short but muscular, dark-haired man. Later, Brian had spoken to Edwards of his earlier life; he was born in England but was the child of an Irish mother and a Spanish father. Educated at a Jesuit college, he had then joined the Army and was, after a short time, posted to the Intelligence Corps. Edwards soon realised that Brian had spent time with the Special Air Service. He was now a free-lance "soldier of fortune." Using his skills with explosives, he had been employed to provide special effects for a number of major films, being made at the famous British Pinewood Studios.

The "little trip," that David Stirling had mentioned to Edwards, turned out to be behind the "Iron Curtain" that then divided Europe between the members of the military alliance of the North Atlantic Treaty Organisation in Western Europe and the Communist Soviet Bloc countries to the east. It was to be to Budapest, the capital of Hungary, a country then within the Russian-dominated Warsaw Pact military alliance. Brian had arranged a series of meetings with Hungarian companies to "talk about various projects." The permission of Edwards's Managing Director to carry out this visit, which was to last a week, was quickly obtained and Edwards's employers would pay for it.

Looking back, it had seemed to Edwards to have been rather a strange trip. Edwards and Brian went off to meet various companies, to talk about projects, which seemed to have little real relevance to Edwards's employers. From time to time, Brian made his excuses and disappeared for several hours, leaving Edwards waiting in the hotel in which they were staying. One evening, they had a drunken and rather riotous dinner with two of Brian's Hungarian friends. Most of the evening was spent in swapping jokes. In rather broken English, the two Hungarians delighted in telling jokes about the Russians. The Hungarians had not forgotten the attempted Hungarian Rising, against their Russian political masters in 1956, when the Russian Army had invaded their country, and killed over 3,000 Hungarian civilians.

It was only after that he had returned to London, that Edwards had realised that he had been used as a "cover" to provide a reason for Brian to visit Hungary, for so-called "commercial discussions." Edwards now realised, that he had only been there to help hide and protect Brian's undercover, espionage activities that he was carrying out in Hungary.

# 5

Only after he had hungrily eaten his dinner did Edwards ask his wife about the Russian phrase; he took the piece of paper Desmond had given him out of his pocket and handed it to her. He described his discussion with Desmond earlier in the day and asked her if she could make anything out of the words on the paper. "It would help if it was in Cyrillic," she said. She tried the pronunciation of the words a few times; to Edwards, each time sounded very different. His wife frowned; "It is not normal Russian," she said. "It is slang and, even worse, I think that it is in a local dialect. You must ask your friend, for me, from what part of Russia the person who spoke these words comes from?"

The next morning, Edwards went to see Desmond and reported what his wife had said. Desmond listened to him very carefully; Edwards thought that he saw a look of amazement in his eyes. "I will try and find out," was Desmond's reply. Another day went by and, then, the following morning Desmond called Edwards to his office. "I have been asked to thank your wife for her efforts," he said. "What we have discussed and what I am going to tell you must be kept in complete confidence, and you and your wife must speak to no other person about this matter in any way. The person who spoke that Russian phrase comes from a small town called Privolnoye in the area known as Stavropol Krai in the North Caucasus." Edwards made a written note of this information.

Edwards took this note back home with him that evening. He told his wife what he had learned; she frowned. "I should have asked you this, too," she said. "Were these words spoken to a person who was born in the same place?"

The next morning, Edwards asked Desmond this question. To his surprise, Desmond answered immediately. "Yes, they were born in the same place," he said. Edwards took this news back to his wife. She thought about it for a while and then she said, "What I need to know now is in what context these words were said. Who were they said about and where?"

Edwards was beginning to enjoy himself; he now felt that this was all about something very important. His wife had done well in beginning to understand this difficult Russian slang, and finding out the local dialect in which it had been spoken, had obviously helped her. He was happy to be part of this effort; he had always hated Communism.

Edwards had been at University in the late 1960's when the radicalisation of student politics had been at its strongest. In the College he had attended, which was part of London University, the so-called Socialist Society had been rampant. It was run by a group of people who believed in the Communist writings and sayings of Marx, Lenin and Trotsky. Despite the fact that the Soviet Dictator, Joseph Stalin, had killed some thirty million of his own people, mainly through starvation caused by his economic policies, they made excuses for him and the continuing brutal Communist regime. These fellow students were arrogant and, if crossed, could even become violent.

Edwards had seen the process of radicalisation at first hand; the leaders of this extreme left-wing group were those who "could afford to be Socialists." Almost all of them had been educated at expensive public schools, were highly intelligent and came from a background of money and privilege. They used others as their "cannon fodder." Usually, these other students came from a poorer background, were generally less intelligent and could be easily led. Edwards was inherently conservative in his views, but he had attended a number of their meetings, just to see what happened at them. In the end, they found out that he was not really "one of them", and that was when the threats against him had started. He had been forced to leave the so-called Socialist Society.

Such was the fervid atmosphere in his College that rumours were common; at various times, certain students were rumoured to be working for the British Security Service, commonly known as MI5, the American Central Intelligence Agency or even the Russian Komitet Gosudarstvennoy Bezopasnosti, better known as the KGB. Edwards believed that he had met a fellow student who was a British agent; he was a former policeman who had given up his job, he claimed, to study for a degree. He appeared to support the current extreme left-wing ideas of promoting an active, even a violent, Socialist revolution in Britain and had taken part in many of the meetings and demonstrations that were held in the College.

But Edwards was suspicious of him, and his general suspicions were compounded when, even his own tutor, had tried to recruit him to the cause! At one of his personal tutorials, this man, who was both a leading academic and an adviser to the Government, suddenly indicated to Edwards that maybe he could help by telling him about some of the more radical students that Edwards knew. At the time, Edwards ignored this comment and, thinking about it afterwards, decided that, he did not really feel that he wanted to begin to "spy" on any of his fellow students.

# 6

Edwards put the further question from his wife to Desmond the next morning. "Is it important that this question is answered?" asked Desmond.

"I believe so," said Edwards. "The Russian phrase you gave me is particularly difficult to translate. It seems that it is in slang, not normal Russian, and it is also in the local dialect."

Desmond nodded. "I will try and get permission to tell you more," he said.

"It seems to me that all this is very important," said Edwards.

Desmond looked at him. "It is," he replied. "But I cannot tell you why. All I will remind you about is Churchill's view of Russia. Churchill said that Russia was one of the most difficult countries in the world to understand."

Driving home that night, Edwards began to realise that he was now part of an effort to find out an important truth. Somehow it concerned Russia and Communism. As well as his visit to Budapest, earlier in his life, Edwards had visited Czechoslovakia. While at university, he had met a Czech girl, who had been admitted to his College after escaping from Czechoslovakia, following the invasion of that country by the Russians and their Warsaw Pact allies in 1968. This invasion had taken place to destroy the easing of hard-line Communism that the new Czech leader, Alexander Dubcek, had tried to introduce and which became known as the "Prague Spring."

Edwards remained friendly with this girl and her new husband, who was a fellow student. A year after he graduated, Edwards, who now had a well-paid City banking job, bought himself a car. He chose a dark blue Citroen which was very comfortable inside and had the unique Citroen Hydropneumatic suspension, which gave a very smooth ride even on uneven roads. This became important when he agreed to go on a holiday to Brno in Czechoslovakia, taking the Czech girl, her husband and another former student friend in his car. The holiday had provided an eye-opening introduction to the real inefficiencies and the total corruption of the Communist political system. His car had proved ideal for the uneven Czech roads, which always seemed to be in a state of disrepair.

Edwards well remembered his first, dramatic sight of the "Iron Curtain," as they crossed from West Germany into Czechoslovakia. There was a very high steel fence topped by barbed wire and regular watch towers, equipped with machine guns and searchlights. There was also a flattened strip of land which, Edwards was later told, was a minefield.

The formalities of crossing from Germany took a long time, but eventually, they were let into the "People's Paradise," as the Czech girl described her homeland. Along the roads were large placards extolling Communism and "Eternal Friendship with the Soviet Union." After about a mile, they came to a second "internal border;" another high wire fence and a barrier across the road, complete with armed Border Guards with large guard dogs. As they were entering the country, they were waved through, but, in answer to Edwards's questions, the Czech girl explained that this second border was to keep ordinary Czech citizens away from the real border and was a further precaution to prevent their escape to the West.

It was at this point in the journey, that Edwards realized that he had made a mistake. He had failed to fill up with petrol, in Germany, before the border crossing. The Czech girl, who was sitting beside him, remained calm. "Just let us stop in the first village we come to," she said. They drove into the first village and, under directions from his female companion, Edwards parked outside the village pub. "Let us go inside and have a beer," she said.

Inside the pub it was very crowded; a large number of the customers were Czech Border Guards in uniform. They carried their machine guns and had their guard dogs with them. The girl ordered beers for the four of them and then disappeared. She came back about ten minutes later. "Don't ask any questions," she whispered into Edwards's ear. "Just give me your car keys and a five pound note." She then disappeared again.

Edwards was more concerned about the loss of his car keys than the money, but she soon returned and they sat and enjoyed their excellent Czech beer. When they had finished their beers, the girl disappeared again for a few minutes, only to return with the car keys. "We can go now," she whispered into Edwards's ear. They returned to the car and Edwards turned on the engine; his petrol tank indicator now showed a full tank. He drove happily on, using what was obviously petrol intended for the vehicles of the Czech Border Guards, who, it appeared, particularly liked collecting Western currencies!

Through the darkened streets of Prague he drove; without the girl, who knew the city well, he would have been totally lost. Before the motorway was built in the 1980's, the only way to reach Brno was along country roads. It took a great deal of time, particularly because of the many road diversions and repairs along the way. At last they reached the house belonging to the girl's parents; it covered four floors and was more than adequate to accommodate them all. They stayed for nearly two weeks, during which time Edwards discovered that the girl's parents were leading members of the local Communist

Party. That was why they had been allowed to keep this large house all to themselves; non-Party members had to share even small flats with other families because of the "housing shortage."

But it did not end there. Her parents were allowed to use special shops, which only Communist Party members had access to; the food that their visitors were served was always nutritious and plentiful. Edwards had visited a local supermarket and had seen the shelves empty of even basic food items. There were sometimes some poor-quality food products available, which the non-Party population had to live on. In health care, Communist Party members had access to specialised hospital treatment and private hospital rooms. For the rest of the population, health care was very much a "hit-and-miss" affair, and, to even see your doctor, you very often had to bribe him. Even when taking holidays, there was a divide; Communist Party members had subsidised access to luxury spas and seaside holidays in Warsaw Pact countries. Party members were more often trusted and allowed to travel abroad to the "West." Special holiday tours to Western countries, were even organised exclusively for Communist Party members.

Thinking back on this holiday in later years, Edwards saw that he had gained valuable insights into the Communist system at first hand. His visit had shown him its lack of freedom, its inefficiencies, its inequality and its corruption. Edwards also found that he had to ask himself the question of why, with such a high standard of living in her home, this girl had come to the "West?" How had she been allowed to escape so easily? Why had it been so easy for her to return? His only conclusion was that she was considered reliable, because of her loyal Communist Party parents, and that she was allowed to leave, in order to spy on Britain and report back regularly to her Communist masters.

# 7

Several days passed at the office before Edwards received a call to visit Desmond again. As always, the call from Desmond's PA came early in the morning. Edwards was free, so he immediately walked to Desmond's office. The proffered cup of good coffee was very welcome. Desmond smiled at him and lowered his voice. "I have spoken to my Friends," he said. "They have agreed that I can tell you more. The phrase was used by a gentleman, made to his life-long male friend, and was about a lady he had just been meeting. They had been talking about a complex and difficult situation. That is all I can tell you." With that part of their conversation over, they continued their discussion about the company's business, and then Edwards returned to his office.

That evening, after dinner, he told his wife, as accurately as he could remember, what Desmond had said to him. She thought for a moment. "I thought so," she said. "I can translate it now."

"What does it mean?" asked Edwards.

"It means," said his wife, "Give her the cake!"

"What?" gasped Edwards, his voice now a whisper. "What on earth does that mean?"

"Don't forget that it is Russian slang," said his wife, "and that it is in the local dialect. It really means, Give her what she wants!"

Edwards got her to repeat carefully her translation. "Remember," she said, "the man who said this to his friend, who was born in the same place, probably thought that nobody else would understand it. Even a Russian from say, Moscow, would not understand what he had said."

Edwards went to bed that night a happy man. The mystery had been solved by his wife, and he now began to see the possible circumstances in which this Russian phrase had been used. He also, he believed, now understood what the implications might be. He could not understand how, somehow, nobody else had been able to translate this Russian phrase. But his wife had been able to do so and he now, at last, thought that he might understand its true importance.

The following morning, as he drove to work, he recalled the visit he had made some years before to Poland. One of his construction companies was building a new hotel in the Polish city of Gdansk. The new hotel was close to the large, Russian naval base. The Russians then used this seaport as the base for their major Baltic Fleet. Edwards remembered the internal flight that he had taken from Warsaw to Gdansk, by the local Polish airline. Standing at the front of the aircraft had been a soldier with a submachine gun. He remained standing during the entire short flight, and was there to prevent any attempt by the passengers to storm the cockpit and hijack the aircraft, in order to fly it out to the "West."

A year before, his company had been digging the foundations for the hotel; one morning they found, deep down, a large buried cable, which appeared on none of the plans that they had been given. The contractors suspended all work on the site and had called the local council to report their find. That afternoon, the Mayor of Gdansk himself appeared, accompanied by a senior Russian naval officer. The cable was pointed out to the Mayor, who was standing on the edge of the large hole.

The Mayor looked down; then he said, in a tone of feigned bewilderment, "What cable? I can see no cable." The following morning, the cable had completely disappeared! The explanation of this episode, reached by the astonished British contractors, was that they had inadvertently uncovered a secret communication cable to the Russian naval base. Such was the "game of mirrors" practised between the two opposing blocks of countries in the "Cold War." The Mayor of Gdansk had been forced to deny the very existence of a very obvious large cable, he could clearly see, but dared not admit to its existence to a contractor from the "West."

As soon as Edwards arrived at his office, he called Desmond's PA and was asked to come along to Desmond's office immediately. As always, as soon as his PA brought in the specially made coffee, Desmond shut his office door. When the ritual of adding the milk and sugar was over, Desmond sat down and looked at Edwards.

"My wife has managed to translate the Russian phrase at last," said Edwards. Desmond sat up. "It is Russian slang, said in the local dialect and probably only understood between these two men. It actually means," he said carefully, "Give her what she wants."

Desmond's mouth dropped open. "What did you say?" he asked in a whisper.

"Give her what she wants," repeated Edwards, beginning to enjoy himself.

Desmond took the small piece of paper from his wallet and carefully wrote down the answer that Edwards had just given him. He sat back in his chair. "That is remarkable, very remarkable!" was all that he would say.

# 8

Some two weeks later, the Prime Minister, Margaret Thatcher, stood up in the House of Commons. She had been asked to answer a Parliamentary Question put to her by one of her own backbench Conservative Members of Parliament. As often, the friendly Member asking the Question had been asked to do so by the Chief Whip, who controlled the backbenchers. The question might even have been written for him, and was to be asked, so that the Prime Minister could make a Statement about the particular subject that was being raised. The Parliamentary Question was along the lines of "Having visited Moscow some months before and having had discussions with the General Secretary of the Communist Party of the Soviet Union, would the Prime Minister now like to comment on her considered view of these discussions?"

The Prime Minister responded with a short and precise summary of the two days of discussions she had attended in Moscow, but commented, "Of course, I do not want to say too much at this stage. Members of this House will understand the reasons for this." But she then went on to say, in conclusion, "that as a result of these discussions, she was pleased to say, that she thought that Mr. Gorbachev was a man that we could do business with." That evening, Edwards was sitting watching the BBC Television News and he saw the recorded clip of the Prime Minister saying these words. He smiled to himself and called his wife to come from the kitchen, so that he could tell her.

In Moscow, the official listeners to the BBC World Service, heard the same recorded clip and carefully made a note of it for their political masters. They realized immediately, that these words of Margaret

Thatcher were very important. They signalled a significant change of attitude by the British Government.

This signal, given by the Prime Minister, led to a growing détente between the "West" and the Soviet Union. Mikhail Gorbachev was able to increasingly follow up on his two new policies of "Glasnost," or openness to new ways of running his country and "Perestroika," or restructuring of the Soviet economy. Gorbachev was now satisfied that he had nothing to fear from the West by following these policies.

A few years later, following certain actions taken and comments made by Mikhail Gorbachev, the apparatus of Communist power within the Soviet Union, and within her Warsaw Pact allies, began to disintegrate. The countries of the Warsaw Pact began to exercise their own political policies, no longer dictated to them by Moscow. The Berlin Wall was demolished, and the "Velvet Revolution" swept away Communism in Czechoslovakia and in the other Warsaw Pact countries.

The individual Republics, within the Union of Soviet Socialist Republics itself, then decided themselves to end Communist rule and the domination of Russia. They declared their wish to be independent from Russia. The Soviet Union, which had been so carefully constructed over many years, would soon disappear into history, and Russia would turn towards a new Capitalist era.

The "Cold War," which had set "East" and "West" at loggerheads for over 40 years, would soon end. It would be replaced by a less frightening reality, where the risk of nuclear war was now reduced and cooperation, trade and commerce could be reinstated between the two opposing "blocks" of countries.

The Russian people and the peoples of Eastern Europe would, at last, taste freedom and democracy, and their standard of living would improve, as resources were shifted from heavy military expenditure to the production of more food and other consumer goods. The correct translation of the words, whispered by the General Secretary of the Communist Party of the Union of Soviet Socialist Republics to his life-long friend and colleague, was the vital proof needed that things were, at last, really ready to change.

# 9

A few months after this announcement in the House of Commons, Edwards received a telephone call from one of the senior Directors of his company. "I understand that your wife speaks very good Russian," said the man. "We are entertaining the Mayor of Moscow to dinner this evening and we would like to invite her along to act as an unofficial interpreter. They are bringing their own, but there is a large Russian delegation coming, and it would help to have an extra interpreter. This is an important event because the Mayor is in office for the next five years and is very well placed to award construction contracts."

Edwards thought quickly. "I am sure that this event will go on until quite late," he said. "I would be worried about my wife being left in London late at night. I will agree for her to come, but only if I am invited as well, so that I can look after her afterwards." The Director seemed unsure. "After all," said Edwards, "I am sure that finance will be needed for some of the construction projects that you will be talking about, and it is on that subject that I know that I can make a contribution myself to the discussions."

So it was agreed that Edwards and his wife should attend the expensive dinner that evening. It was held in the private cellar room of a luxurious but small hotel in the West End of London. A long dining table had been set up with a spotless white table cloth and napkins. The scene was completed with silver cutlery, flowers and sparkling cut-glass wine and water glassware. Being underground, the room was lit by clusters of candles, which gave an intimate and rather luxurious feel to the proceedings.

Edwards had heard stories about this room; it led into the hotel's wine cellar where many fine wines were stored on a series of racks. Some of these bottles dated from before the Second World War and commanded a very high price. At the end of the cellar, was a blocked-off section, which was once a secret tunnel between this room and Saint James's Palace. There, the Royal Family had often taken refuge during the German bombing raids of the last war. So this arrangement had once been an escape tunnel, in case Saint James's Palace had itself been bombed.

The Russian guests arrived shortly after their hosts; Edwards and his wife were kept a little in the background but were eventually introduced to the Mayor of Moscow and his delegation. The Mayor's face lit up as he was greeted by Edwards's wife in Russian. He spoke just a few words of English and obviously was delighted to find that one of his hosts spoke his language. Thinking about this evening afterwards, Edwards had to ask himself, why was it that Desmond, who also claimed to speak Russian, had not been invited to this important event? Was the answer, perhaps, because his real background might have been already known to their Russian guests?

After pre-dinner drinks and a tour of the wine cellar given by the hotel's Senior Wine Steward or Sommelier, they were seated at the table. Edwards was delighted to find that he was seated opposite the Mayor of Moscow. His wife, further down the table, was in great demand to translate the statements being made by the senior Directors of Edwards's company who were present. Edwards managed to exchange a few remarks with the Mayor about how he could help in finding finance for new construction projects.

After a long and delicious meal, complemented by the finest wines, coffee, liqueurs and cigars were served. The Mayor of Moscow promptly stood up and, in the Russian tradition, began to propose a series of toasts. Edwards's wife translated each one carefully. At the third toast, following that to our British hosts and to continuing Russian-British friendship, the Mayor locked his eyes on Edwards. The toast in Russian was quite long; Edwards's wife remained silent.

"What did he say?" asked Edwards.

"I don't know whether I should really translate it," said his wife. "He proposed a toast to the most important man in the room; to you. He called you "Mr. Money" and said that, without your help, nothing will happen!"

After the dinner, the guests and hosts mingled in the reception area of the hotel to say goodbye. Edwards, wisely, he thought, paid a visit to the lavatory in view of the long journey home. When he returned, he found the Mayor of Moscow enthusiastically embracing his wife. He held her very tightly, kissing her on both cheeks, then on both hands. He was whispering, quite loudly, into her ear. A long flow of Russian words was pouring out of him. "What is he saying?" asked Edwards, a little jealously.

"He is complimenting me on my excellent Russian and on my deep understanding and obvious love of the Russian people," replied his wife.

Edwards smiled quietly to himself. If only the Mayor of Moscow had really known the truth, of what his wife had recently done, to so very much improve British-Russian relations!

THE END

# The Byzantine Bridge

-

*"If one had but a single glance to give the world, one should gaze, on Istanbul."*

**— Alphonse de Lamartine**

# 1

"We have been keeping you under very close observation," said the man.

Edwards was sitting opposite him on a hard wooden chair. Behind him, back from the action, sat Jones from the Marketing Department. It was Jones that had insisted that Edwards attend this late evening meeting. They had taken a taxi and then Jones had guided him through a maze of city streets and down various narrow alleyways.

Finally, they had found the right door and climbed a rough, uncarpeted staircase to enter this bare room. The man sat behind a cheap desk on which there was a brass desktop lamp. It was the only light in the room and the man had angled the lamp purposely, so that it shone straight into Edwards's eyes.

From what Edwards could see, the man was dressed in a dark blue blazer and grey trousers. He had not stood up when Edwards and Jones had entered the room. Edwards had proffered his hand, when he had introduced himself, but it had not been shaken. The man had a sallow face, short black hair and hooded eyes. Edwards noted the bulge under his left armpit. When the man leaned forward, his blazer opened a little and Edwards saw the unmistakable glint of an automatic pistol contained within a shoulder holster!

"You arrived in Istanbul on the seventh of last month on the British Airways flight which landed at 1330 hours," continued the grim-faced man. "You then took a taxi to the Hilton Hotel, where you checked in to Room 205. In the afternoon, at 1530 hours, you had a meeting at the offices of the Turkish construction company that you are working with. It was with the Chairman and Managing Director of that company. In the evening, you had dinner with the Second Secretary at the British Consulate in Istanbul. At a fish restaurant on the Asian bank of the Bosphorus. You paid for this meal using your American Express card."

Edwards swallowed hard and shifted in his uncomfortable chair. He looked back at Jones, whose face had turned ashen; he looked very scared. The harsh, monotonous voice droned on, in good English but with a strong, Turkish accent. The voice continued to give an exact and accurate description of Edwards's last, completed visit to this, the largest city in Turkey.

Edwards knew now that Jones's brief description of this man was accurate. Jones had said that this man had served in the Turkish Navy and that he had risen to the rank of Commander. He had then joined the internal Turkish Security Service. He had claimed that he was now the senior bodyguard to the Turkish Prime Minister. Jones had also briefed Edwards that this man's good friend was the Mayor of Istanbul; he had been photographed with the Mayor at numerous social occasions.

"It is all Jones's fault," Edwards thought to himself. Just three months ago, Jones had asked for a meeting. Edwards now worked for a group of construction companies and was responsible for giving them general financial advice and for finding finance, when that was needed, for projects that they wanted to undertake, both in Britain and overseas. One of the companies that Edwards looked after was recognised as one of only three companies, in the world, that was capable of building major suspension and cable-stay bridges. This company had been a member of the British, German and Turkish consortium of companies that had built the first suspension bridge over the Bosphorus at Istanbul, thereby joining Europe and Asia.

This had been back in the mid-1970s, and now, ten years later, in 1985, Jones had excitedly told Edwards that their Marketing Intelligence indicated that the Turkish Government was about to ask for competitive proposals, from companies around the world, to build a second suspension bridge, on a site just down the Bosphorus from the first bridge. Jones had already travelled to Istanbul, to meet with what was then the largest Turkish construction group, to consider them as a possible partner to work with. In this way, he had hoped his company could win the contract for this new major project. Could Edwards please now visit Istanbul, meet with this Turkish company and then confirm Jones's view that they were the right people to work with?

Edwards had flown to Istanbul and had stayed at the Hilton Hotel. Exploring the hotel on his first day, he discovered that it had a rather exclusive shop, on the ground floor, selling a great variety of Turkish Delight. "I must visit here to buy a present for my wife, before I leave," he had thought. He had met with the Chairman of the construction group and his son, who was the Managing Director; this leading Turkish family owned the company.

They had entertained Edwards to dinner on his second evening in Istanbul. They owned a large, elegant, corporate mansion on a hill, with spectacular views over the Bosphorus, and this is where they entertained their guests. Beneath glittering chandeliers, an excellent dinner, complete with fine wines, had been served. A pianist had played over dinner, on a grand piano, in the corner of the large, ornate dining room. After dinner, they had taken their coffee, cigars and digestives out onto the balcony. From there, there was a magnificent view, as the sun set over the Bosphorus.

Despite this fine entertaining, Edwards had given careful and objective consideration to this family firm, before he approved of Jones's choice of business partner. While the company had the undoubted ability to help in the construction, what had decided Edwards, in the end, was something that he had been told by a senior banker in London, who, Edwards knew, had worked on Turkish business for many years. This intelligence was that the family, who owned this construction company, had been the major financial contributor to the Motherland Party, which had recently won the General Election in Turkey and now formed the government.

Edwards was now waiting for the Commander to come to his main point; he had convinced Edwards that he was well aware of the results of the total surveillance placed on Edwards while he was in Istanbul. But what did this man really want? The man began talking of his great friendship with the Mayor of Istanbul. "You will be aware," he said, "that in our country, it helps to have people that will help you. Of course, they will only help you if they themselves are done a favour. I am sure that my good friend and I can help you to achieve your goal."

So that was it! This man wanted to arrange for a bribe to be paid to the Mayor and himself to help Edwards's company get the contract! But Edwards was not sure that this man was really in a position to help. Instead, he believed, that the final decision, would more likely be made by the Turkish Government in the capital city of Ankara, rather than by the Istanbul city authorities. Edwards had to think very quickly about his reply, but he did not want to offend this frightening man.

"Tell me," he said. "I understand that you are very close to the Prime Minister and that you indeed are the most senior person responsible for his personal safety?"

The man looked at Edwards carefully. "That is correct," he replied.

"Your Prime Minister was recently in London," continued Edwards. "Were you with him in London fulfilling your duties of leading his Turkish security detachment?" The Commander nodded. "I assume that you liaised closely with our Metropolitan Police and our Security Service in doing this?" asked Edwards.

"Of course," replied the Commander.

This time, Edwards nodded and then changed the subject. "You will understand," he said, "that I will have to consult with my senior colleagues regarding your offer of help. Thank you for that kind offer, but I will have to get back to you as soon as I can with the views of my colleagues."

The Commander nodded. "I understand, of course, that you will have to consult with your colleagues, Mr. Edwards," he said.

"It has been a pleasure to meet you this evening," Edwards replied, standing up to indicate that the meeting was at an end. This time, the Commander stood up and shook hands, in farewell. Edwards, followed by Jones, descended the steep wooden staircase. Once outside, Edwards took some deep breaths. The fresh air smelt very good!

# 2

Edwards and Jones retired to the bar of the Hilton Hotel for a drink. It seemed that Jones's nerves had still not recovered. "However did he know all those things about your last visit?" asked Jones. "Well, it is easy to check the incoming passenger lists at the airport, if you are in his position," replied Edwards. "Then you can check the guests registered at a hotel. After all, you have to show your passport here when you check-in and they take a copy of the photo page. Once they know what you look like, it is easy enough to arrange for you to be followed. I suspect that they may also have an agent, within the Turkish construction company that we are working with, so they can check what is happening within it."

Jones seemed amazed, but Edwards appeared blasé about their meeting that evening. "I have travelled to Eastern Europe several times," he told Jones. "There, the Communist authorities usually want to know what you are doing. So you can be monitored and followed by their Secret Police everywhere." But Edwards had noted the situation carefully. For some reason, his presence in this city and his movements were under surveillance. It was difficult to know why that was; it might be that the Commander had deployed his "watchers", under some pretext, merely to impress Edwards. That way, he could then, more easily, demand a bribe for himself and his friend, the Mayor of Istanbul, to "help make things go the right way."

They had now signed a formal agreement to work with the Turkish construction group, after he had recommended them, so that they would provide the essential local input, such as labour, and basic materials, such as cement. This would be a very large construction project; not only would it include the new bridge but also a new road system, on both sides of the Bosphorus, to funnel the heavy Istanbul traffic over it. As a result, his company were thinking about bringing other companies into their consortium. There had been a German contribution to the building of the first bridge, and discussions were now starting, with a major German company, to help design and build the new roads that were required. As an overall Project Manager, to ensure that this major project was delivered, within the time and price agreed with the Turkish Government, his group had already approached a major American company. They had a very good reputation in this kind of overall management activity.

His group company would work on designing and building the bridge alone. The German company would work on the roads and the Turkish company would provide the local input for both the roads and the bridge. Each company would therefore have a role, but it was bringing all this together, successfully, that really mattered! Edwards was already aware that his consortium of companies had international competition. Amongst those rivals, was a Japanese company, which was one of the other companies in the world capable of building a major suspension bridge. They had teamed up with an Italian construction company that specialised in building the roads required and with another leading Turkish contractor to provide the "local content." This increased the pressure on everyone to work fast and accurately, when putting their complex bid together, for this project.

For Edwards, bringing the construction consortium together properly was an issue to be dealt with by other people in his group. His main role was to concentrate on finding the finance. The Final Bid proposal, which had to be submitted to the Turkish Government, in a few months' time, had to be a firm, fixed-price one. It had to be accompanied by a Finance Package. This had to provide finance to the Turkish Government, for the full amount of the fixed price that was being offered and cover the cost of building the new bridge and the new roads that were to be built at both ends. This Finance Package would include an element of export credit from each overseas country involved.

By now, most exporting countries had an Export Credit Agency, supported, in one way or another, by their government. These agencies provided government loans or guarantees to finance overseas buyers for a large part of the goods and services exported from their respective countries, at quite favourable rates of interest. The British had their agency and so did the Germans and the Americans. To the total amount of export credit available, would have to be added a separate "commercial loan" from a consortium of banks, who would take the risk on the Turkish Government, rather than on the governments of the exporting countries. This commercial loan would have to be offered on the best terms available, and added to the export credits, so that the full amount of the quoted price for the project was fully covered by finance. The Finance Package was a major international exercise in itself, and Edwards had already spent a lot of time and thought on it.

He had considered a number of banks to lead this "Banking Consortium." It was necessary, because of the export input from various countries, for the participating banks to be truly international. They had ideally to be represented in each participating country of his company's consortium, by means of a branch network, or own a bank resident within the country concerned. They had also to be capable themselves of a major participation in the "commercial loan" element of the finance required. He would have to use the export credit element of the total package, which would be guaranteed by the respective governments and was therefore an attractive piece of banking business, as an incentive for the banks involved, to also provide the required "commercial loan" element, which was not guaranteed by the governments of the exporting countries, but by the Turkish government alone.

"There is no such thing as a free lunch!" was the expression that came to Edwards's mind. Having said that, he was offered a number of free lunches by a variety of banks that were anxious to lead, or just participate in, the banking consortium for this major and prestigious project. He also had to consider the other construction companies involved in their contractors consortium, and consult with them about his choice of the banks that they would jointly use to support their combined bid.

In the end, he made the decision to go with a major American bank as the leader of the "banking consortium." It had both a branch network in Turkey, and it owned a separate Turkish registered bank. It had recently led a consortium of major banks for a previous "commercial loan" to the Government of Turkey and could therefore easily repeat this operation. It was capable of providing the export credit, supported by the American government, for the goods and services that would be exported from the United States. This bank, agreed to bring into their "banking consortium," the British and German banks that would benefit from the British and German parts of the government-guaranteed export credit loans. These Edwards had carefully selected, after they had agreed to provide their respective parts of the necessary "commercial loan," which would have to be provided to the Turkish Government on attractive banking terms, for the balance of the bid.

The American bank, leading the banking consortium, had also agreed to provide any missing balance of "commercial loan" required to be made to the Turkish Government, on the same attractive lending terms. In other words, they had agreed to "underwrite" the whole of the "commercial loan" which was a risk directly on the government of Turkey. After a lot of work, Edwards, at last, had his banking consortium put together and work could now begin on finalising the figures and terms for the various loans. To do this, of course, estimates of their final prices, from the various participating construction companies for their share of the construction work, had to be obtained and a national breakdown of sources of equipment, materials, labour and services worked upon.

# 3

The work on and coordination of this Finance Package would take Edwards many months, starting from his first visit to Turkey. But the initial choice of banks and their roles had now been completed. Now the details would have to be filled in. Back in his office, overlooking the busy flyover in West London, Edwards had time at last to think. How was he going to react to the clandestine meeting that Jones had taken him to? The man he had met had known so much about his movements in Istanbul, that it had been frightening. This knowledge, it seemed, could only have been obtained, if he really was a senior member of the Turkish Security Service. His closeness to the Mayor of Istanbul made Edwards uneasy. But, he had put an offer to help on the table, for a price, of course. That final price would still have to be negotiated. But did he really have the power that he claimed?

Edwards stood up, walked over and closed the door of his office. As he did so, he smiled at his loyal Personal Assistant, Liz, who was sitting at her desk, just outside his door. "I have to make a confidential call, Liz," he said. "I will only be a few minutes."

He returned to sit behind his desk. Edwards reached down to the bottom, left-hand drawer of his desk; now he always kept this drawer locked. Inside the drawer was a black folder which he took out and put on his desk. Inside the folder, were some sheets of paper, with various names and telephone numbers written on them. Alongside each name were the names of various countries. These were the contact details of various experts on these countries, whom Edwards had met over the years and whom he now consulted, in strict confidence, when he needed to do so. Fortunately for Edwards, they all seemed willing to talk "off the record" to him about these countries and the various leading personalities in the commercial and political worlds within them.

But on one small, yellow piece of paper was a special telephone number; it had no name or country beside it. He had been given it some years before, and he had been told to use it only when it was really necessary. It would be answered as "Under Secretaries Department, Foreign and Commonwealth Office." But Edwards knew that it was a direct line to the British Secret Intelligence Service, more commonly known as MI6. He rang the number and knew that some special equipment would immediately identify the caller and check the line for any surveillance taking place on it.

He identified himself. "I have recently met a Commander Vardar of the Turkish Security Service," he said. "I understand that he is the senior bodyguard to the Prime Minister of Turkey. The Prime Minister was here recently, and Vardar confirmed that he was with him. He was in charge of his Turkish security detachment, so, I assume, that he would have liaised closely with the Metropolitan Police and with our Security Service. Is it possible for you to check, please, whether you know Vardar and also to get confirmation that this liaison with him actually took place?"

He did not expect to hear back for several days and was surprised when, the following morning, his direct line telephone rang. "Foreign and Commonwealth Office here. Under Secretaries Department speaking," said the anonymous voice on the other end of the line.

"You asked about a Turkish gentleman," it continued. "A Commander Vardar?" Edwards confirmed that he had indeed done so. "I am sorry to say that we can find no trace of this gentleman," the voice continued. "He was not part of the Turkish Prime Minister's party when he recently visited London. Unfortunately, he is not known to any of our agencies."

Edwards thanked the voice profusely and replaced the receiver. "Caught you out lying," he thought to himself. "I do not think that we will be using you to help us; you have no real power in Ankara." He decided not to formally reply to the "Commander," but to leave the matter unresolved, which would keep the other man guessing. He would have to tell Jones of both of his decisions. After all, in international business, you wanted to minimise the number of enemies that you made and you did not want people, you had formally turned down, to start working against you!

But this was not the end of matters of this kind. A few weeks later, he received a call from the secretary of the Group Director to whom he partly reported. The man wanted to meet Edwards in his office the following day. Edwards did not like this man; he was a bluff Northerner and had a belief in his own self-importance and infallibility. When they met at the headquarters of the group in Central London, he told Edwards that he had been contacted by a Turkish businessman, who had successfully bought and then built up a British company. The Turkish businessman had offered to help them win the contract for this project if he could, and the Group Director asked Edwards to go and meet him in his offices.

Edwards discovered that this man's company had offices in the East End of London and arranged to meet him there. On the day, it proved to be a long Tube journey and then a very long walk to find the right building. Having identified himself, he was shown up to the man's plush office suite on the top floor of the building. He was received politely and given an excellent Turkish coffee. But the businessman seemed to want first to talk about himself and to tell Edwards how successful he had been. He explained how he was making most of his profits by growing various crops in Turkey and paying his workers very little in Turkish Lire, which was, in any case, a weak and depreciating currency. He then exported the crops, mainly by air, and was paid for them in harder currencies, such as the Pound Sterling.

At last, their conversation turned to the project in Istanbul that Edwards was working on. "You realise that I have very good contacts with the Government of Turkey," the man started to say. "I think that I can use these to help your company win the project. Of course, it will cost you something, but you will be able to add that amount to your price, so the effect on your company will be neutral."

Edwards began to probe with some well-placed questions. "Who would you talk to on our behalf?" he enquired first. From the answer he received, it seemed obvious that the Turkish businessman had not yet properly thought through the senior people that he would contact. Just to be sure, Edwards tried to approach his question from a different direction. "Which of the current Turkish Ministers do you know well?" he asked. Again, the man did not answer this question to Edwards's satisfaction. He tried again with a few more probing questions but failed to receive a proper response.

The meeting had already lasted for over an hour and Edwards decided to bring it to an end. "I will, of course, have to discuss this with my senior colleagues" he said. "Thank you for your time today. I will try and contact you again when we have had the chance to discuss this matter internally." The man understood, nodded and smiled. They shook hands and Edwards was shown out of the building by the man's secretary. On the long walk and Tube journey back to his office, Edwards mulled over what had happened over the last few hours.

Back in his office, Edwards made his decision; he was not at all convinced that this man had the contacts or indeed the ability to help them win the contract. Maybe he had thought, that he could negotiate and receive a "success fee," if they won the contract, when, in fact, he had done very little to help them achieve this success. It was often very difficult to set up these kinds of arrangements and to prove that anyone had really made any difference to the final outcome.

To make himself sure of his conclusions, Edwards decided to call one of his banking contacts, who specialised in Turkish business. In strict confidence, he told his contact about the meeting. "Do not touch him," was the immediate reply. "I know that he is already under investigation both here and in Turkey, for various financial matters that I cannot go into." Edwards thanked his banking friend and then called the secretary to the Group Director to set up a meeting with her boss for the following day.

When they met, the Group Director seemed very unwilling to accept Edwards's conclusion about the Turkish businessman. Only when Edwards mentioned the confidential view that he had received from his senior banking contact, did the Group Director grudgingly accept what Edwards was telling him. But the Group Director insisted that Edwards go back to the Turkish businessman with a formal response, rather than just make no further contact, as Edwards had recommended. Edwards explained again, that he thought that silence was the best policy; that way they would not make "a possible enemy" of this man and have him perhaps acting against their efforts.

But, in the end, Edwards had to accept what the Group Director wanted. "I will telephone him and politely decline his offer of help," said Edwards. "I will think about what I will say very carefully and try and find a rational excuse that I can make to him." In any case, he knew, from what he had been told, that this Turkish businessman was already a "busted flush." If he became annoyed with Edwards's firm, it probably would make no difference, whatever he tried to do, as it probably would not work.

# 4

The date when their Proposal, or bid, had to be made to the Turkish Government, came ever nearer. Edwards worked with his relevant colleagues, in the Turkish, German and American companies, to finalise certain financial items to be included in the consortium's price. Payments, which had to be included in the price, for the costs of providing export credit to the Turkish buyer, had to be calculated, based upon the amounts of the relevant goods and services that would be financed by this method. The banking fees for issuing various types of bonds required by the terms of the construction contract, such as a performance bond, guaranteeing the consortium's work, had to be included. So, too, had to be the insurance premiums, paid to cover the unfair calling of such bonds, and other types of risks that the contractors might face, and which could be covered by the insurance market.

The bid price had to be submitted in United States dollars, and so the risk of movements in exchange rates against the other currencies, required to carry out the contract, had to be considered over the three year period that this project would take to complete. Because it had to be a firm, fixed-price bid, no increase in prices for inflation could be allowed. Therefore, any expected increase in the prices of goods and services, to be provided over the three year construction period, had to be included in the fixed price. An advance payment would be made by the buyer, followed by a series of stage payments, as various milestones in the work were reached. These had to be carefully worked out, so that the contractor's cash flow always remained positive and the contractors did not have to fund progress themselves.

All this, and a lot of other information, had to be collected into a set of financial projections, to make sure that this major contract would actually pay for itself, and produce a profit for the contractors, at the end of the project. It was important, that the contractors would not be forced to find finance for themselves, and that the work could be continued uninterupted. When the date for the bid submission was only two weeks away, it was agreed that all the contractors involved, would each send a small team to Ankara to coordinate and finalise the complex process of the bid submission.

So, a week before the bid was due to be submitted, Edwards found himself on a flight to Ankara, as part of a team representing his company. It was led by the Group Director to whom he partly reported. It included, also, the Managing Director of the bridge-building company that was part of Edwards's construction group.

Ankara had been made the new capital city of Turkey in 1923, by Kemal Ataturk, the founder of the modern Republic of Turkey. Ataturk was a senior Turkish Army officer, who, following the defeat and dissolution of the Ottoman Empire during and immediately after, the First World War, rose to power. He defeated the victorious Allies' attempts to partition mainland Turkey between them, and became the first President of modern Turkey.

Ankara had been a place of human habitation for thousands of years, but nearly all of its buildings were now modern. Most of the employment in the city was related to government activity, but it was also an important industrial and commercial city, located at the centre of Turkey's road and rail network.

Edwards's team joined the teams from the Turkish, German and American companies who had also arrived in Ankara. They met in the local offices of the Turkish construction company. The Turkish Chairman had given his employees, who normally worked there, a week's paid holiday so that their offices would be available for the international teams. The offices consisted of an open area, with about a dozen desks, a small Director's Office, which the Turkish Chairman now occupied, and two small meeting rooms which were used as "break-out" rooms for individual teams to meet in, when they needed some privacy. There was also a reception area with some easy chairs and an overworked coffee machine.

They all worked exceptionally hard each day, from eight o'clock in the morning until eight o'clock at night, including over the intervening weekend. Food was brought in for lunch, and the late dinners, at their respective hotels, in the evening, were usually used as opportune planning sessions, for the work to be carried out the next day. On the day before the bid was due to be submitted, the Turkish Chairman announced that, for security reasons, so that their final bid price could not leak out, everybody would now be locked into the building, until their final bid had been submitted to the Government, the following morning. They worked hard, straight through the night, to complete their bid.

Edwards well remembered the lingering smell in that open plan room; it was a mixture of cigarette smoke, strong Turkish coffee and human sweat! Edwards had occasional sessions, in one of the small meeting rooms, with the relevant, financially orientated people from the other companies. He regularly met, also, with members of his own company team, in the other meeting room. More informal, smaller meetings and discussions could take place in the reception area. In between these times, he wandered from desk to desk. Each desk allowed for one or two people to be seated, with other team members standing around.

By nine o'clock in the morning, their joint bid was finally agreed and completed. It was contained within two sealed envelopes; one contained their fixed bid price for the construction project and the other had inside it the final financial package that Edwards had completed.

The Turkish Chairman announced that his car and driver were outside waiting for him to take the envelopes to the relevant Government office before the deadline of eleven o'clock that morning. Everyone was now free to leave the building for their hotels for their breakfast and a good rest. Although very tired, the senior members of Edwards's team and the other company teams, remained behind to await the Turkish Chairman's return. They wanted confirmation that, indeed, their final joint bid had been successfully submitted and had been officially accepted, by means of a signed, timed receipt.

The Turkish Chairman arrived back and announced a successful submission. "I will be flying to Frankfurt tonight on the company jet," he announced. "I will then get it to fly on to Heathrow Airport. I can take five more people. Can you decide between you who those will be? I will then arrange for cars to collect you all, from your hotels, at five o'clock this afternoon to take you to the airport." It was agreed that the senior representative of each of the British, German and American companies would travel back in this more comfortable manner. The German would be dropped off in Frankfurt, with the Turkish Chairman. The other two seats available would be taken by Edwards and the Managing Director of the British group's company that would build the new suspension bridge. They would be flown on to London with their Group Director and the senior American representative.

They all returned to their hotels for a meal and some badly needed sleep. At five o'clock that afternoon, the three British representatives were collected from their hotel and driven to the small terminal at Ankara Airport that dealt exclusively with private jets. There they met up with the Turkish Chairman and the senior American and German delegates.

The Turk led the group through the building; a Turkish Immigration official tried to stop them and asked for their passports. The Turkish Chairman said a few gruff words in Turkish to him, and he waved them on, without any check. They marched across the tarmac and boarded the small jet aircraft. Inside there were six very comfortable executive-style seats and two pilots, waiting to take off immediately. Edwards saw a large box, sitting in the middle of the floor. Once the jet had taken off, the co-pilot came back from the cockpit, and opened it. Inside were six bottles of Moet & Chandon Dom Perignon Champagne, on ice!

# 5

The passengers on the corporate jet from Ankara grew more and more animated. Edwards found that he needed something to eat, to help offset his consumption of alcohol. At his request, the co-pilot brought out a supply of some luxury crisps and nuts.

"Have you no other food on board?" asked Edwards.

"No, sir," replied the co-pilot.

There was general laughter around the cabin. "You are always thinking about your stomach!" commented his Group Director.

"I think that, by the time we reach Frankfurt, we shall all be very hungry," replied Edwards.

"Radio ahead and order four first class meals to be brought on at Frankfurt and some wine to go with them," said the Turkish Chairman to the co-pilot. "Now gentlemen, I want all of you, in turn, to use the radio telephone here, on my plane, to call your wives, wherever they are. Give your home telephone numbers to the co-pilot and he will connect them to you."

Edwards was lucky; his home telephone number was one of the first to be connected and he spoke briefly to his wife. He explained that he was on his way home earlier than expected. When it came to his Group Director, there was no reply at his London home. "Oh, she is not there. Try my country house instead," he pompously requested. Again there was no reply. Laughter spread around the small cabin and some ribald comments were made.

"She's probably out with the milkman tonight!" the Managing Director of the bridge-building company shouted at his Group Director, who did not seem at all amused!

At Frankfurt, the small jet aircraft disgorged a drunken Turk and a drunken German. It then flew on to Heathrow, where it landed just before the airport closed for the night. The remaining four passengers on board, had all hungrily eaten their first class dinners, that Edwards had sensibly requested.

Two weeks after this jolly return from Ankara, Edwards was called to a meeting with the Finance Director, to whom he also reported. Once again, Edwards took a Tube train into Central London, to the Group's headquarters, which were close to one of London's famous squares. At least, he had respect for this man and looked forward to their meetings. He was a Chartered Accountant by background, and extremely professional in the way that he treated people.

"We have just heard the results of our bid to the Turkish Government from the Chairman of the Turkish construction company," he told Edwards.. "We have been beaten into second place behind the consortium representing the Japanese bridge-building company and the Italian construction group, who will build the roads. Their final bid was one hundred and twenty-five million dollars lower than ours."

"But we all know how the Japanese work," replied Edwards. "They put in a low bid to start with and then claim further money, as they go along, as a result of unfortunate but necessary amendments to the contract. But, by this time, it is too late for the client to change contractors."

"I know that," said the Finance Director. "But we will never be able to convince the Turkish Government that this is their game. Instead, the Board has decided that you must go back to Ankara and convince the Turkish Government that they must not borrow any more Japanese Yen. The Japanese have priced their element in Yen and provided financing in Yen, which is, in any case, non-compliant with the terms of the bid, set originally by the Turks. But the Turkish Lire is depreciating against the Yen and, I think, will continue to do so. If they accept the Japanese bid and their Yen loan, it will cost the Turkish Government a lot more just on the alterations in the exchange rate, between those two currencies, over the long period of time involved."

"Am I allowed to alter the price after I consult back with you in London?" asked Edwards.

No way," replied the Finance Director. "You can emphasise that we have put in a firm, fixed price for the work to be done, but that is all. You must go out there and convince the Turks to accept our bid, and in this way, they will not have to borrow more Yen, which will become more and more expensive for them to repay."

"What about our Turkish partners? Can they not help too?" asked Edwards. "I believe that they have very good contacts with the Turkish Government."

"That side of things will be handled by the Group Director," was the reply. "He believes that he has a very good rapport with their Turkish Chairman. Just keep me informed of what is happening out there, and I will inform him."

"But I think that this is a very difficult task," said Edwards.

"I know," said the Finance Director. "But this is the only thing that we think might succeed. Incidentally, the Turkish Government was very complimentary about our finance package, which you put together. They thought that it was much better than the one that was submitted by the Japanese and Italian consortium."

"So you want me to go straight away and do this on my own?" asked Edwards.

"Yes," was the reply.

Edwards stood his ground. "It could be a long and difficult visit," he said. "I want someone with me."

The Finance Director looked at him; he could see that Edwards was determined. "Who do you want?" he asked, rather grudgingly.

Without too much hesitation, Edwards replied, "Henry!"

"Why?" asked the Finance Director.

"Because Henry has the kind of mind that could be very useful in this kind of tricky situation," Edwards explained. Edwards did not tell the Director what he knew about Henry's history. Henry had been a small Jewish boy, in Prague, just before the Second World War had started. He had been allowed, by the occupying Germans, to leave his native city on one of the trains organised by Sir Nicholas Winton, to bring such young, Jewish children safely to England. Arriving here, he had been adopted by a family in Portsmouth, only to lose his adoptive family, as a result of a German bomb falling on their house, while Henry was at school. Then he had been given to a second English family to be brought up.

After the war, Henry had found out that his parents and all his siblings had died in a Nazi concentration camp. Henry spoke about five languages fluently, including Czech, Russian and German, and had gained a lot of experience in trying to sell behind the "Iron Curtain" in the now Russian Communist-dominated countries of Central and Eastern Europe. His mind was incisive and sharp, and he was used to working under pressure.

"Ok. Henry will go with you," conceded the Finance Director.

Three days later, Edwards was returning to Ankara; his group's travel agency had booked Edwards and Henry adjoining seats on the flight out, and the pair had agreed to meet in the British Airways Business Class Lounge at Heathrow Airport. Edwards had arrived first; he was now a little tired of Champagne, so he poured himself a gin and tonic at the bar, instead. He sat down and tried to read a copy of the *Financial Times*. But, his mind was much troubled by this visit which, he had already described to his close colleagues, as another "Mission Impossible."

Suddenly, he saw Henry; he had his overcoat on and his lank fair hair was brushed back. When he saw Edwards, a great grin came over his face and he waved and started to walk towards him. There was one strange thing about Henry today; he was carrying a violin case!

"Whatever have you got there?" asked Edwards.

"I have brought my sub-machine gun," replied Henry, grinning even more widely. "It will be useful to get rid of the opposition." He placed the case on a table, clicked the locks and opened it. Inside sat a beautiful violin; its varnish gleamed in the overhead lights. "It is a late eighteenth century instrument, produced by a Czech master maker," said Henry proudly. "But it is mine. I saved up over the years to buy it, and now I want to play it on every occasion I can."

Edwards smiled at him. "That's another thing that I did not know about you, Henry," he said. "I did not know that you played the violin."

The two colleagues sat together on the aeroplane, but, they knew better, than to talk business. You never knew who was sitting in front of you or behind you and who could hear what you were saying. Instead, they talked about music and about families. Edwards's first child, a daughter, had just been born, while Henry's children were older. Edwards was very pleased to receive some parenting tips from

Henry. Towards the end of the flight, they started telling each other some stories. Henry's were usually about his exploits in countries behind the "Iron Curtain." He told one story to Edwards, which Edwards had heard before, but he did not tell Henry that he had already heard it, as it was well worth repeating.

One day, Henry had been negotiating with a senior Communist Party member, who had now become a Government Minister, in Henry's beautiful, native city of Prague. A few minutes after leaving this man's office, to walk back to his hotel, Henry had realised that he was being followed. He entered a nearby bar, and used the public telephone, there, to call this man.

"Why have you sent someone to follow me, Vaclav?" he asked.

"Where are you, Henry?" was the response. So Henry told him which bar he was in. "Just stay where you are and have some drinks on me," was the reply. "I will send someone better to follow you."

For a few moments, Edwards played with the amusing idea of contacting Commander Vardar and introducing him to Henry. Then Henry could give the Commander the benefit of his own surveillance experience!

# 6

Ankara sits on a high plateau in Anatolia, but is surrounded by a bowl of mountains. It has lengthy, snowy winters, and when they arrived, winter was already approaching. The air was cold and crisp, but the air quality was not helped by the thousands of wood and coal-burning stoves, that the population of some five million people, used to keep themselves warm. As their taxi entered the city from the airport, Edwards and Henry noticed the smell of smoke in the air and the fact that smog was beginning to gather around the buildings. They arrived at their hotel; somehow the travel agency, used by their group, had booked them into a "Government-owned" hotel. It was a tall, gaunt building, and the décor inside was Spartan and cold.

They checked in and ascended in the lift to the tenth floor, where they had been given adjoining rooms. Their rooms were plain and cheaply furnished. Edwards had begun his unpacking, when there was a knock on his door. It was Henry. "Let us go for a short walk," he said. Edwards looked at him strangely; he could not work out the reason behind Henry's request, but he complied with it. As soon as they were outside, walking around the block, Henry turned to him.

"You realise that the whole hotel is wired for sound," he stated. "I don't like the hotel, and we will be listened to all the time, I am sure. Let us try and find somewhere more comfortable and secure."

Edwards agreed, but then he had an idea. "Can you give me a violin recital tonight, Henry?" he asked. "Unless you are too tired, after the journey," he added thoughtfully.

It was by now freezing outside, so they quickly returned to the hotel. That evening, they had dinner in the hotel dining room; the service was nearly non-existent and the food was awful. Afterwards, they went back upstairs to Henry's room. They sat closely together on Henry's bed, while Henry played his violin. In whispered tones, they talked to each other about the tactics that they would adopt to deal with the Turkish Government. When Henry took a rest from playing, they talked only about music. Then Henry resumed his excellent playing.

"This is better than standing in the bathroom, with the taps turned on, so that they cannot hear us!" Edwards joked quietly with Henry.

Within a few days, Henry had found another hotel, and they thankfully moved in. It was small and owned by an Austrian couple. From the outside, it looked rather like a large Austrian chalet that you would find in the mountains of the Tyrol. Inside, it was decorated and furnished in the same Austrian style, all in a homely fashion. "The German word for this is gemütlich," said Henry, well satisfied with his choice.

Their first meeting was with the British Embassy in Ankara. The size of their construction group, and the importance of the project they were working on, was such, that they had received an invitation to visit the Embassy as soon as they could. They first met the Commercial Secretary and were then introduced by him to the Ambassador. The Ambassador was charming and helpful; he had a pronounced limp. "A problem with a German bullet during the Second World War," he explained. "Why don't you come here for dinner with me tomorrow evening and we can discuss tactics?" Edwards and Henry readily agreed, and the following evening, they were provided with dinner at the Embassy.

They explained carefully to the Ambassador and the Commercial Secretary, who was also present, the full details of their project. Then Edwards explained the "Mission Impossible" that he had been given. The Ambassador looked at him shrewdly. "The people who run this country now are the Ozal brothers," he explained. "Turgut Ozal is the Prime Minister, and his brother, Yusuf, is now the Minister for Planning. You need to get to both of them, but you must also meet up with other relevant Ministers or their senior officials. I will do my best to help you and try and arrange a program of meetings for you. Tomorrow evening, there is a Reception at the Ministry of Planning.

I have been invited, and I will try and get you an invitation. That will give you the opportunity to meet Yusuf Ozal. I will call your hotel tomorrow morning and let you know if I have been able to get an invitation for you."

The message came through from the Ambassador the following morning; an invitation to the Reception that evening would be delivered shortly to Edwards's hotel. So, in the evening, Edwards took a taxi to the building housing the Ministry of Planning. The large room was full of diplomats of various nationalities; in quick succession, Edwards met the American and French Ambassadors. Then he spotted the British Ambassador on the other side of the room.

"Come with me," said the British Ambassador, once Edwards had joined him. "Let us try and find the Minister." Soon they found him, and the Ambassador introduced Edwards and explained why he was visiting Ankara.

The Minister smiled. "Your visit here has been anticipated," he said. "Ambassador, please call my Secretary tomorrow morning and set a time to see me tomorrow. We will then deal with this formally, with my senior officials present."

"Thank you so much, Minister," said the British Ambassador politely. Then to Edwards he said, "Be at the Embassy at nine o'clock tomorrow morning, so that we can go and see the Minister when we are called." The Ambassador wandered off to talk to some of his fellow diplomats, but Edwards stayed. He had found that the Minister was not only highly intelligent, but also spoke excellent English. He started talking to the Minister about what was happening in Britain with privatised projects; how the British Government was now asking the private sector to build, own and finance major projects which, up to now, had been financed by the Government.

The Minister smiled again. "I think that we might have been there first," he commented. "When my brother and I took over, we found that a very large contract for a nuclear power station had been given to an American company by the previous government. But we knew that the country could not really afford this project. We also knew that, for diplomatic reasons, we could not cancel the contract. So, instead, we asked the American company to own and finance the project themselves. We knew, of course, that they could never find the finance for the very long period required to pay off the major loans required for a nuclear power station. The project would, therefore, never happen!" Edwards had to smile at the very clever way, in which these two brothers, had solved this problem that they had inherited, on taking office.

The next morning, Edwards and Henry reported to the British Embassy at nine o'clock. They were given a message; the meeting with the Minister had been set for eleven o'clock and they were invited to leave with the Ambassador in his car at twenty to eleven precisely. Meanwhile, they were invited to have coffee with the Commercial Secretary. At the appointed time, the Ambassador collected them. Outside the front door of the Embassy, his official car, a Rolls-Royce of course, was waiting with the Ambassador's driver at the wheel. Edwards walked to the other side of the car, so that the Ambassador could get in more easily. "No, Mr. Edwards," said the Ambassador firmly. "I always sit on that side, behind the flag." He indicated the Union Jack, that fluttered proudly from the front right-hand wing of the car.

At the Ministry, they were immediately ushered in to see the Minister, who was flanked by his two most senior officials. The Ambassador made the introductions and then "turned the floor over" to Edwards to explain why he was there. Edwards, as clearly as he could, explained the problem that the Turks might experience, if they accepted the bid and the finance package from the Japanese/Italian construction consortium. The financial burden would probably increase for the Turks in terms of the Japanese Yen, and its continuing increase in value against the Turkish Lire. He also said that the price that the British-led consortium had submitted was a firm, fixed price. He added that the Japanese had a history of going in with an initial low price and then adding to it, with contract amendments, as they went along.

He then made his own comments on the competing Japanese/Italian finance package, which he believed that he could do, as this was his expertise. He had prepared and finalised the finance package for his own consortium's bid for this project. He thought that, while the Japanese Yen part of the finance was available, the finance needed for the Italian road component of the work, and the remaining balance of finance needed as a commercial loan to complete the package, had not yet been approved and therefore, was not yet confirmed and available. The Minister replied that he "had made a careful note of the views expressed and that he would, most certainly, consider them."

The meeting ended and they returned to the Embassy car. On the back seat, the Ambassador sat behind the flag, with Henry between him and Edwards, as they returned to the Embassy. The Ambassador turned to Edwards. "Tell me," he said. "I was a little confused in there about what you said about the Italian finance. Can you explain it again, please?" By now, Edwards had mastered the art of "diplomatic speak"; he gave an answer to the Ambassador, that carefully skirted around the subject, without actually saying very much. The Ambassador looked puzzled; Henry leaned forward between them. "What he means to say, Ambassador," he said, with a cheeky grin on his face, "is that the Italians have not got the bloody money!" The Ambassador smiled; he now understood exactly what Edwards had been trying to tell him.

# 7

In their new hotel, Edwards and Henry now felt free to talk to each other openly about the major problem that they were facing; how could they convince the Turkish Government to accept their consortium bid that was one hundred and twenty-five million United States dollars more expensive, than that of the Japanese/Italian consortium? With the help of the British Ambassador, several further meetings with Turkish Ministers were arranged. One morning, they visited the Ministry of Finance and were met by the Deputy Minister of Finance himself. Again, Edwards put forward his arguments about Turkey borrowing more appreciating Japanese Yen to fund a Japanese-supplied bridge.

That afternoon they met with the Minister of Public Works, to whom the competing bids for this project had been submitted. The Minister of Public Works was surprisingly honest with them. "Gentlemen," he said, "I am afraid that the difference in your price, is just too much to compensate, for any possible rise in the value of any additional Japanese Yen borrowing, that we might undertake." Edwards explained to the Minister, that their price was a firm and fixed one, whereas, the Japanese had a history of submitting low initial bids and then escalating the price later with contract amendments. But this idea was not accepted by the Minister. "I am afraid that your price is just too high," he said.

"If only we were allowed to lower the price, even if only by a little," muttered Edwards to Henry after the meeting, as they returned by taxi to their hotel. After these two frustrating meetings, they decided to call London. The time difference of three hours meant that Edwards managed to speak to the Finance Director, who had sent him on this "Mission Impossible", just before he left the office. He explained the reactions that they were getting and how they needed to lower their price, if only by a token amount. "I am sorry," was the reply, "I am afraid that I cannot authorise you to lower the final price we have arrived at. That was the best, fixed price that we could offer the Turks. Anything less than that, and we will make a loss on the project."

It was at this point in his telephone conversation, that Edwards suddenly noticed something. There was some music faintly playing in the background! He realised, straight away, that their telephone call was being listened to in a rather amateurish way. Just to check, he suggested to Henry that he call his wife from the telephone in his own room and listen to see whether that call was also intercepted. A few minutes later, Henry came back to Edwards's room.

"Yes, I heard it too," he said.

"So the Turks are listening to our telephone calls from here," said Edwards. "But they are not very good at it, are they? I would have expected something better from them, and that they would not let us hear that they were listening to a radio while they were waiting for our calls."

Henry smiled and looked at him. "You are making an assumption there," he said. "What if they wanted us to know that they were listening to our telephone calls?"

"So it is a game of Cat and Mouse," said Edwards. "I understand now. But surely, now we know that they are listening to us, we can play dumb and use that to our advantage?"

"How?" asked Henry.

"Well, part of the "intelligence game" is that they do not want their political masters to get a nasty surprise. So we can play with them and let them know the things that we want them to know. The rest we keep to ourselves." Henry just nodded.

So, every afternoon, Edwards and Henry sat down and agreed what they would tell the Turks. Then, every afternoon, at the same time, Edwards would call London and tell their London-based colleagues and the listening Turks, the things that they wanted the Turkish Government to know!

They had now established a routine; every other day at ten o'clock in the morning, they took a taxi and arrived at the British Embassy to have a meeting with the British Ambassador at ten-thirty. The Ambassador had insisted that he always be kept fully briefed on what they were doing and wanted a report on each meeting that they had attended. He also wanted to know what reactions they were getting from their London headquarters. He would tell then them what he was picking up from his continuous contacts with the Turkish Government. Edwards and Henry informed the British Ambassador about the telephone surveillance that they were experiencing; he merely shrugged his shoulders and indicated, in his words, that "it was just par for the course."

Every time, for this regular Embassy meeting, they were conducted to the most secure Chancery Department of the Embassy. They were then shown into a particular room, where the Ambassador was waiting for them. However, it was a special room, containing yet another room, which had inside it, just a table and some chairs, for a meeting to take place. This second room was made from a special glass, impregnated with a fine, wire mesh. It was a so-called "Faraday Cage," specially designed so that no words spoken inside could be intercepted, by any known form of advanced electronic surveillance.

One morning, they were seated within this "secure room", when the British Ambassador looked at them. "Yesterday, I carried out another round of enquiries, with senior people, that I know, in the relevant Government Departments here," he said. "Everything I was told indicates, unfortunately, that we are getting nowhere with our arguments. The big problem is the difference between your price and the price offered by the Japanese and Italian consortium. The Turks just do not believe that any upward movement in the Japanese Yen, affecting their further borrowings of that currency, will compensate for that difference in price. You tell me that your company is unwilling to reduce their price, so, I cannot see, what else can be done."

"I understand, Ambassador," replied Edwards. "I think that the only thing that is left, that we might do, is to send a message at the highest level."

The Ambassador's eyes fixed on him. "Do you mean from our Prime Minister to their Prime Minister?" he asked.

"Yes," replied Edwards.

The Ambassador pushed a pad of paper towards Edwards. "Write it, then," he said.

So Edwards wrote a letter from the British Prime Minister to the Turkish Prime Minister. He tried to keep it as short and concise as possible but, at the same time, to mention everything that he thought was essential. He tried a first draft, read through it and made a few alternations. He then added a couple more sentences at the end. Then, in case of any mistake, he rewrote the whole letter as a second draft and read it through very carefully. Finally, to be sure, he read all the way through it again. The Ambassador and Henry just sat and watched him. At last, he was satisfied; in any case, he thought, the Prime Minister's advisers will alter anything that they do not like. He pushed the pad back to the Ambassador, who did not even look at the draft. "I will get this out to London immediately," said the Ambassador. "Please be back here at ten- thirty tomorrow morning."

That evening, Edwards and Henry ate an excellent dinner in the small dining room of their "Austrian chalet." Edwards smiled at Henry; he had earlier had the pleasure of telling his Finance Director in London and the Turkish listeners that a message from the British Prime Minister was on its way!

"I am missing the sound of your violin, Henry," he said. "Will you give me a short recital this evening please?"

"Of course," replied Henry, and for the rest of their meal, they discussed the music that Henry would play. It was so pleasantly relaxing for Edwards, to sit back and just listen to Henry's excellent violin playing. Also, not to have to talk to him, at the same time, in muted tones as he had had to do at their previous, "wired-up for sound" hotel.

# 8

Precisely at ten-thirty the following morning, Edwards and Henry arrived back at the British Embassy in Ankara. Again, they were shown into the Embassy's secure room, where the Ambassador was waiting for them. "This has arrived from Downing Street overnight," said the Ambassador and handed Edwards a telex message which had been deciphered. Edwards read it through carefully. Only a few words had been altered from his original draft. At the bottom was the name of the British Prime Minister, Margaret Thatcher. "I have a copy, now typed in a proper letter form, ready for the Turkish Prime Minister," said the Ambassador. "We keep a facsimile of the Prime Minister's signature in the Embassy which can be attached. First thing this morning, I set up an appointment with Mr. Ozal's office, to deliver this letter personally to him. I am due at his office at eleven o'clock. Mr. Edwards, would you like to come with me, so that I can introduce you?"

This time, the Ambassador sat firmly behind the British flag and just Edwards was sitting beside him. Edwards was surprised by the attention that their car received; as the gleaming Rolls-Royce, flying the Union Jack, passed through the streets, people stopped and stared at the car. They soon arrived at the Turkish Prime Minister's residence at the Cankaya Mansion in the Cankaya district of Ankara. The Ambassador and Edwards were quickly conducted into the Prime Minister's outer office, where they sat and waited.

Then, the Prime Minister himself opened the connecting door, and invited them to enter his private office. He, of course, like his brother Yusuf, spoke good English, and the Ambassador politely presented the letter to him from the British Prime Minister. Only a few words were said about the project, but Edwards managed to get in a concise statement of his main arguments. That over, the Prime Minister stood up, shook hands, and then personally ushered them out to the corridor. There, they were joined by a Turkish Army Officer, who escorted them back to the British Embassy car.

"I think that was quite satisfactory," the Ambassador said to Edwards, as soon as their car moved away. "Now let us see what happens."

"I do not think that you, or we, can do much more," replied Edwards. "And I must thank you so much for all you have done. Now, because I have other work to do, I must think about returning, with Henry, to London. I assume that what will happen now, is that the Prime Minister will consult with his other Ministers, and then formally write a response to our Prime Minister."

"That is correct," said the Ambassador. "I assume that now there will be a few days of silence, before a formal response is made."

That evening, over dinner, Edwards told Henry about the meeting at the Cankaya Mansion. "I do not think that there is much more that we can do here," he said. "Like you, I have other projects to work on back home. I think that, tomorrow, we should turn our open return air tickets into a flight back to London in the next few days." Henry agreed with this, and the following morning they called the Finance Director, on the telephone. He agreed with their request to return home. They had, after all, already been in Ankara for nearly three weeks. Later that day, they both made a last visit to the British Embassy to formally thank the Ambassador, who had been so supportive during their stay. The following day, they took the British Airways flight back to London.

Back in his office, Edwards had a large amount of urgent work to attend to and a further pile of routine matters which needed replies.

Fortunately, the faithful Liz had sorted his work out for him, into urgent and non-urgent paper piles. There was also a long list of telephone calls to be returned and some invitations to lunch and other events to respond to.

When he had any spare time to think, Edwards mused about his trip. He could not see how he could have done any more, given the constraint he was under, about not changing the price. He made contact with a senior civil servant, whom he knew well, at the Department of Trade and Industry. Edwards had, personally, fully briefed him on the project before he had left for Ankara. He knew that this man would be copied in with any "signal," or message, from the British Embassy in Ankara about the project.

A full week went by, before he heard anything; one morning, his direct telephone line rang. It was the senior civil servant. "We have received a "signal" from Ankara," he said. "It enclosed a formal reply to the Prime Minister. I am afraid that it is bad news. The Turks have decided to accept the Japanese and Italian consortium bid, despite your hard efforts. The difference in price between your two bids was just too much. I will be sending you, in confidence, a copy of this "signal" shortly."

Edwards thanked his civil service contact; he would wait until he had the copy of the full text from Ankara before he informed the Finance Director and the Group Director. The bad news would then be sent to the Managing Director of their bridge-building company, and to the other companies in their construction consortium.

So Edwards had to mark down the conclusion of this "Mission Impossible" as a failure. But that was not the end of the story. The contract was signed between the Turkish Ministry of Public Works and the companies within the Japanese and Italian consortium. They took some time to start the work; as Edwards had suspected, the non-Yen part of their finance package was not ready. Several months went by, until the Italian Government, were at last persuaded to provide their guarantee for the export credit finance for the exports of goods and services, that would be coming from Italy.

It also seemed to prove difficult to complete the commercial loan element of the deal; the Japanese and the Italians had to work very hard, to complete the offer of bank loans for the full amount of their contract price. In the end, the rate of interest and the fees on these loans had to be increased, to encourage the banks involved, to make the full required amount of the loans available.

Edwards was now fully engaged on other projects, but the bridge-building company, within his group, were carefully monitoring what was happening with the building of this major new bridge in Istanbul. Some years later, he met with the Managing Director of the bridge-building company, on another project. This was the man who had accompanied Edwards on the merry flight on the private plane back from Ankara. Their talk turned to that event and to the experience that they had all gained, from working on that project.

"Did you ever hear what finally happened?" asked the Managing Director.

"No, but please do tell me," responded Edwards.

"Well, we are still talking to the major Turkish construction company, that we were then working with," was the reply. "They tell us that, with the delays in starting the project, because of the lack of a properly finalised finance package, the Japanese have had to throw everything at it to finish the new bridge on time. As a result, there have had to be a whole series of contract amendments which, somehow, they have persuaded the Ministry of Public Works to agree to. I suspect that, there have been some very large "private inducements" given out, to get them to agree to all of these!"

"I would not be at all surprised to hear that," said Edwards, and he grinned at the Managing Director. "Bribery there is just par for the course," he added.

But, for the Turks, worse was to come; as predicted, the Turkish Lire continued its decline in value, while the Japanese Yen continued to appreciate. So the additional borrowing, denominated in Japanese Yen, that the Turkish Government had agreed to take on, became an even heavier burden for Turkey to repay. But, finally, when the bridge and the new roads, on both sides of the Bosphorus, were at last completed, with all the contract amendments that had been agreed and had taken place, the final price proved much higher than the original Japanese/Italian consortium bid. Extra finance, for the Turkish Government, in Japanese Yen and United States dollars, had to be found to meet this increased price.

It was calculated, that the final price of the Japanese-supplied bridge was some three times the price that had been originally agreed upon. The Italian-supplied roads came out, finally, at twice the price signed up to by the Turkish Government in the construction contract. The Japanese had been successful in their trick of submitting an initial low "fixed" price, and once the project had started, the Turkish Government had been "locked into" the process of expensive contract amendments, unable to change contractors in the middle of such a major project.

These large increases in prices eclipsed, many times over, the original price difference between the bid prices of the Japanese/Italian consortium and the British-led construction group of companies.

This final price also showed the effect of all the extra bribes, received by certain Turkish Ministers and officials, but then, of course, included in the ongoing construction costs. It had turned out not to be the cheapest "firm, fixed price bid," offered to the Turkish Government, after all!

## THE END

# On the Road

-

*"Never, ever, forget History."*

— **Kusno Sosrodihardjo Sukarno,
First President of Indonesia.**

# 1

"You do realise that I could have you stopped at the airport. You would never leave the country!"

Edwards stiffened and sat upright in his comfortable chair. He looked across the low glass-topped table, at the person who had just said these words. On the table were two steaming cups of coffee that had just been brought to them. He had made the mistake of telling his host, that he would be returning to London at the end of the week. He knew that they were perfectly capable of doing what they had just threatened. Their dark brown eyes were watching him carefully, to see his reaction to these words. He shifted uncomfortably in his chair. He swallowed hard, and thought very carefully about what he would say next. His whole future might depend upon it!

It had all started nearly a year ago, in 1987. One morning, he had received a call in his office from the secretary who worked for the Group Director, to whom he partly reported. She requested him to come to a meeting with her boss that afternoon at three o'clock. After lunch, he had taken a London Underground train and then walked to the building that was the headquarters for the large construction group that he now worked for. His job was to provide financial advice and, when needed, raise finance, for a variety of different types of projects, both in Britain and overseas.

These projects were those that were of interest to a growing portfolio of construction and engineering companies, owned by this parent company that he was just about to visit. Their building was close to one of the "London Squares"; the areas of green that provide a "lung" for Central London. This particular Square had once been immortalised in a song about a nightingale. He showed his pass to the security guard at the door and took the lift up to the second floor.

Edwards did not like his current Group Director; he was a bluff Northerner with curly red hair. Edwards has once seen him reduce a grown man to tears by criticising his work! Then he had placed his arm around the man's shoulders and told him quietly to get out of the meeting room, that they were in, and start again on working out the estimated costs of the major project that they had all met to discuss. Edwards knew him to be a bully and to be highly opinionated. He never had any regard for what other people were telling him and often laid down his own decisions, without properly listening to the advice that he was being given.

Edwards could not but compare him with his predecessor; he had been a charming Scotsman who had originally recruited Edwards to his current job. He had acted as a Group Director for some years, before leaving to take up the role of Chairman of a Regional Development Authority. Eventually, he had been rewarded with a much-deserved knighthood. Edwards always said about him, that, "After you had a meeting with him, you consistently came out of his office, feeling much better." From Edwards, this was a rare compliment!

As always, Edwards had to brace himself as he was shown into this current Group Director's office. You never really knew what to expect. "I have a project for you," growled the man, not even lifting his eyes from the papers he was examining. "I recently met the President's daughter, and she has been given this project to do by her father. But they need to have the finance put together for this project, and that's your job." He rudely thrust the papers, in his hand, over to Edwards. "Read these and let me know what you think."

The meeting was clearly over. Edwards returned to his office, the same way that he had come. His office was situated in a tall, red-brick block in the west of central London. It was situated next to a major traffic flyover, and even with its thick windows, the sound of the constant, heavy, passing traffic, could never be muffled out

Edwards carefully studied the papers that he had been given. They were in English, but they concerned a proposal to be submitted to the Government of Indonesia, for the building of a toll motorway to link the capital city of Jakarta with Bandung, the second largest conurbation on the island of Java. Unusually, this was not a project which the Government would be funding. It was to be funded by the company putting forward the proposal, and they would then be repaid and continue to benefit from the ongoing profits, from the receipt of the tolls paid by the traffic using the motorway.

A similar privatised arrangement had recently been introduced in Britain, by the then Conservative Government, to fund the building of a new toll bridge, over the River Thames, at Dartford. This new bridge, would form a vital link for the M25 motorway, which encircled London, and therefore, the estimated future income stream was considered to be both large and highly likely to be achieved.

But this project was in a distant foreign country, the income stream was unknown, and might be subject to uncertainty. Edwards decided that he needed some help. The next day, he contacted people who worked in three leading merchant banks and requested an urgent meeting with the relevant Director or Manager, who he spoke to. He knew that they all dealt with finance for major construction projects. But also they were all aware of the new demands, for some of these projects, to be "privatised" and funded in other ways, than by governments. Rather than talk to his Group Director, he left a message with his secretary, to let him know what he was now doing.

Over the course of the next week, he paid a visit to these three leading banks, which were all located in the financial centre of the City of London. Each of them had an interesting history; they had been founded in the late eighteenth or early nineteenth century by German or American immigrants to promote trade between their countries and the United Kingdom. Some of the leading merchant banks had been founded by prominent Jewish families, such as the Rothschild's, and they all now specialised in the areas of corporate advice, international finance and the managing of large investment portfolios for pension funds, insurance companies or high-net-worth individuals.

These merchant banks were known for their expertise, creativity and entrepreneurial spirit, and they were staffed by both the children of aristocratic families and, increasingly, by the brightest and the best from leading English universities, such as Oxford and Cambridge. Edwards met with people, whom he already knew, in each merchant bank that he visited. He had chosen them carefully, because he knew them as both highly experienced and creative individuals. Each one was already involved in the area of "privatised" projects, where various governments were now looking to the private sector to finance and build major projects, and then repay themselves, from the income received from these projects.

In each bank, he was well received, and he spoke, in strict confidence, about the project that he had been given in Indonesia. He was then asked for the time, for each of them, to study this new project, as they all wished to seriously consider it. But, in each case, he was eventually told, that this project was impossible to finance. At the end of this series of consultations, he called the Group Director.

"I have tried three leading merchant banks," he said, "but they have all said that this project cannot be financed. It is deemed to be too uncertain."

"I don't care," was the curt reply. "It is your job to do it. Get on with it!"

So Edwards had to set out on his latest "Mission Impossible," as he now called such challenges. He had been given similar tasks before, and speaking to his colleagues, he had remained philosophical about this new project. His only comment to them was, "The Impossible can be achieved today. Miracles can take a little longer."

# 2

The Singapore Airways "Big Top" Boeing 747 aircraft was pushed off its stand by the small tractor, and started to taxi, under its own power, towards the main runway at Heathrow Airport, ready for take-off. The top deck was given over exclusively to business class passengers, and Edwards liked this arrangement. Up there, he was away from the rest of the passengers and, as far as possible, away from the noise of the four large Rolls-Royce jet engines.

As soon as he arrived at the terminal, in a taxi from his home, he had been made to feel important. The special check-in desk had a strip of red carpet leading up to it and was for first and business class passengers only. He was directed through a special "fast track" channel for security and then easily found the business class lounge, where he could wait in comfort. The only problem was the long walk to the departure gate, but ordinary passengers had already boarded and there were no delays, waiting in a long queue, to board.

Inside the aircraft, he climbed the winding staircase to the top floor, deposited his carry-on bag in the space provided, and was shown to his very comfortable seat, with its copious legroom. Immediately, the pretty, Chinese air hostess, in her long, colourful sarong, welcomed him on board with a large smile. Then, at once, she brought him a glass of excellent Champagne, on a silver tray.

Edwards believed in dressing smartly to travel; if you were well dressed, you were shown respect at airports and on the aircraft. Only once had that failed to work; on his first flight to New York, which was full of his fellow university students, he had made the mistake of dressing smartly. On his arrival in New York, he had been singled out by Immigration Officers and closely questioned about his background and intentions in visiting the United States of America!

The smiling hostess handed him a bag containing some of the essentials for his flight; a pair of earphones for the in-flight entertainment, a toothbrush and toothpaste, cosmetics to prevent dry skin, a comb and various other items, including a pair of over-socks. Edwards gratefully took off his shoes and pulled on the over-socks. He knew that his feet would expand during the long flight and that he would have difficulty getting his shoes back on, when they arrived. But, even a small shoe-horn was provided in the bag, to help in that task. Meanwhile, wearing the over-socks, was well worth the comfort.

He fastened his seat belt and prepared his mind for take-off and the thirteen-and-a-half-hour non-stop flight to Singapore. He had purchased a newly- published paperback by one of his favourite authors, not available to non-air-travellers, in the "Airport Specials" section of the bookshop, that he had passed on his way to the departure gate. He knew that he would not read much on the flight, but it would be available for him to read, if he had any spare time, during his trip abroad. It was a "gift to himself" to help recompense him from being away from his family for over a week and a reminder of home. "Another glass of champagne would help," he thought, and within a few minutes, he had been brought a second glass!

The very long flight was broken up by excellent meals, served on the finest bone china, with silver cutlery provided. A menu was presented to him before each meal, and he could choose from, at least, three main dishes on offer. The food was tasty and excellent, complemented, of course, by fine wines. After the meal, coffee and digestives were brought; he chose his favourite 10-year-old single malt whiskey. An Eastern malt; he did not like the heavier and smoky Western malts, which usually came from the islands off Scotland.

After watching one film from the on-board library, he tried to sleep. Despite the offered blanket and the eye mask, that blocked out all the light, he found that he could never sleep properly on an aircraft. He was awakened for breakfast with a large, heated face towel and the choice of fresh fruit, juices, cereals and a full English breakfast. If preferred, a lighter Continental breakfast was available. Several more glasses of Champagne were provided to complement the breakfast. "The only proper way to start the day!" Edwards thought to himself.

At Changi Airport, he carried his bag off the aeroplane; it contained everything that he needed. He did not like the wait at a baggage carousel, when you arrived at your final destination, or the thought of the shock, when one's suitcase failed to appear! He had heard of people's cases disappearing for a few days at this airport, while the Singapore Intelligence Service opened and searched their suitcases, for any information on what these businessmen were doing in the region. As a transit passenger to Jakarta, he did not have to pass through Immigration, and after a stop at the airport's book shop, he found his way to the comfortable Silver Kris Business Class Lounge for the one-hour wait, until he could board the short flight to Jakarta.

As he sat and waited, reading some of the local newspapers available, he promised himself that, on his return flight home, he would take advantage of the excellent Duty-Free Shopping Centre, that occupied a large part of the departure area. Soon he was in the air again, crossing the Equator, to land at Soekarno-Hatta International. The terminal here was built in the shape and style of a Javanese long-house; it was a long walk through the terminal, but soon he was through Immigration and Customs and then into an air-conditioned taxi bound for the Mandarin Oriental Hotel.

The Mandarin Oriental is located in the financial and diplomatic centre of Jakarta and is recognised as the most luxurious hotel available in this city. Jakarta, known to its inhabitants as "The Big Durian", after the evil-smelling Durian fruit, was founded in the fourth century, but captured and then expanded by the Dutch in the seventeenth century, as the capital of their Dutch East India Company. It was known then as Batavia. While the city itself now had some ten million inhabitants, the population of its total Metropolitan Area was closer to thirty million.

Edwards's taxi was lucky; it missed the morning rush hour with its inevitable traffic jams and was soon driving around the large roundabout, with its fountain and winged statue, outside his hotel. The car door was opened, his bag taken and he was conducted into the large, marbled foyer. The necessary signed form and passport check over, he was escorted to his room on the tenth floor. Gratefully, he kicked off his shoes and lay down on the large double bed, which was covered with an ornate bedspread. He looked at his watch, which he had set to the correct local time, as he had landed. He calculated the difference in time from London. "Exactly twenty-four hours since I left home in the taxi for Heathrow," he thought.

That evening he would have a dinner meeting; after a light snooze, he got off the bed. He unpacked, showered, put on his pyjamas, pulled the curtains shut and had a proper sleep. For lunch he ate some snack biscuits he found next to his well-stocked refrigerator, and then decided to get dressed. He took the lift down to the ground floor and wandered around, looking at the in-house restaurants and the expensive hotel shops. He changed some traveller's cheques for the local Rupiah currency at the reception desk. Then he went and bought a local newspaper, which was printed in English, from the hotel's newsagent.

He took the newspaper back to his room and started to read it, sitting on one of the comfortable chairs provided The sooner that he began to understand this vast country, with its two hundred and sixty million people, and its three thousand islands, strung out in an archipelago over three thousand miles in length, the better!

# 3

His guest at dinner that evening was the local representative of "The Noble House." Under a long-standing agreement, this organisation provided advice and support to Edwards's group of construction companies. "The Noble House," was the local Hong Kong name for Jardine Matheson, by then a large multinational conglomerate, but which had been founded in Canton, as a trading house, in 1832 by two Scotsmen, William Jardine and James Matheson. However, the firm moved to Hong Kong in 1842, when the British were ceded Hong Kong Island by the Treaty of Nanking, following the defeat of China in the First Opium War. The two founders had already made a fortune out of the trading of tea, other commodities and opium with China.

It was this trade in opium, which was destroying the health of a large part of the Chinese population, which caused a series of wars with the British, who, of course, claimed that this evil export to China should be part of their "free trade" policy. This policy had to be defended, at all costs, and therefore, war was declared on China, when it refused any further opium imports. The antiquated Chinese Navy was totally destroyed by a small number of British Navy vessels. As background reading, Edwards had purchased a book at Changi Airport by the British historian, Maurice Collis. He had been asked to write the official history of Jardine Matheson, but, when they saw the completed book, the firm had tried to stop publication.

It was eventually published in 1946 under the title "Foreign Mud". This was the name that the Chinese gave to the processed opium, that they were being forced to import. The book told the true story of the Opium Wars and how this illustrious company had made a fortune as very successful "drug dealers". A contact had recommended to Edwards that he should read it, to understand better this aspect of the history of South East Asia. However, the book had been banned in Hong Kong, and it was now out of print in Britain. However, it had been republished in 1980 in Singapore, where Edwards had bought it at Changi airport.

Roger was a charming man; over a long dinner, Edwards got to know him. A product of one of the better British public schools, then an officer in one of the Guards regiments, Roger had spent many years in South East Asia. For the last seven years, he had lived in Jakarta. In confidence, Edwards told him about his "Mission Impossible"; he realised that Roger's help and advice would be invaluable. For his part, Roger seemed to be very willing to help Edwards in any way that he could.

.

Roger was in great contrast to the previous representative of "The Noble House" whom Edwards had met. On one of his visits to Hong Kong, Edwards had been asked to meet one of the Directors of Jardine Matheson. His name and title showed that he was the Chief of a Scottish clan. He took a taxi from his hotel to the tall building, on the edge of Hong Kong Island, overlooking the great harbour. The name Hong Kong, translated from the local Cantonese dialect, means "Fragrant Harbour", although, with the vast amount of shipping now using it, it was no longer very fragrant.

The Jardine Matheson building is unusual in having large circular windows like a ship's portholes. In the local Cantonese dialect, it is called "The Building of the Thousand Cunts!" Whether this local name referred to its round windows, or to the people inside the building, was still unclear to Edwards?

Edwards remembered his journey, in the special lift, up to the top executive floor of this building. A receptionist took him down a long corridor, lined with ancient Chinese paintings. He was shown into an outer office where he met the man's personal secretary. When he was ready to receive him, she opened the great double doors to the inner office, so that Edwards could meet the "Great Man."

It was a huge, richly furnished and ornately decorated office. At the far end, Edwards could see a little figure sitting behind a vast desk. As he advanced across the room, the rich pile of the carpet seemed to get thicker and thicker. It seemed to Edwards that he had to struggle to make the last twenty to thirty feet of the carpet. He was welcomed with a rather grudging handshake. Who was this lower-class Interloper, who dared to disturb the "Great Man's" day?

Roger quickly arranged for Edwards to meet some more people; one of them was a representative from the Dutch Embassy in Jakarta. "They still know a lot about what goes on here," Roger had said, "and I know and trust this man to give you the best advice." Edwards met the Dutchman at his Embassy; only after the meeting, did he realise that he had been speaking to a senior Dutch Intelligence Officer, whose information and insights into the politics of Indonesia, were to prove most useful.

Edwards was treating his first visit to Jakarta as an "information-gathering exercise." As well as Roger's contacts, he tried to meet some senior bankers and other British professionals, such as locally resident lawyers and accountants, to gain as much knowledge of the local business conditions as he could. It was essential also to have a first meeting with the Indonesians he would be dealing with. The "First Daughter's" company, that was submitting the proposal for this toll motorway project, was in an office building not far from his hotel. He had arranged to meet the "team" of relevant people over coffee, one morning, in their offices.

He took the lift up to these offices on the auspicious eighth floor; the number eight is considered to be lucky in South East Asia. He was surprised when the lift doors opened. The decoration was certainly Indonesian, with highly colourful Javanese figures placed in the corners of each room and Indonesian art on the walls. But the overall decor was in pale pastel shades. He soon understood why. He was received by four people; one of them was a male lawyer, and the other three were young and attractive Javanese ladies! This was a company mainly staffed by women, and the colour scheme of their offices, perfectly reflected that fact.

It was now nearly a year after his first visit, and he had visited these offices many times. The dark brown eyes were still watching him for his reaction to the threat that had been made, to stop him at the airport, from leaving the country. The eyes were set in a beautiful, oval, Oriental face. Her jet black hair fell to her shoulders, and the exclusively cut Western dress she wore, could not hide her voluptuous figure. Edwards was sitting opposite the Personal Assistant to the eldest child of the President of Indonesia. He had been told that she was also a Princess from a Royal House that had for centuries ruled over an ancient city in Central Java. Whenever he referred to her, with his colleagues, he now called her "The Princess."

He swallowed hard and then smiled at her. "I know that you could keep me here," he said. "But if you did that, we would not be friends anymore, would we?" His gamble worked; a lingering smile came over her face, and he knew that he had won her over. They went on to talk about the progress that was being made on the motorway project and planned their next steps. As well as business, this attractive woman, now had sufficient confidence in Edwards, to talk to him about her personal life, and indeed to ask his advice on several matters outside business. What she said to him outside business matters he, of course, kept in total confidence.

That morning, rather than take the short taxi ride, Edwards had walked to these offices from his hotel. He had found his way through the back entrance of the hotel, through the hotel gardens and then out onto the pavement. Care was needed in walking along the pavement, which, in places, was uneven and wet from the overnight rain. Care was also needed, as the pavement was treated as an extra traffic lane by many riders of scooters and motor-bikes! They came tearing up behind Edwards as he walked, and he stood aside, so that they could overtake him. The other pedestrians were very friendly; they waved and smiled at him, as if it was no surprise seeing a white man in a business suit, shirt and tie, carrying a briefcase, taking a rather hazardous walk in the humid heat of their city.

Edwards smiled and waved back enthusiastically. For his part, he liked this short exposure to local life, away from the cocoon of his hotel room and air-conditioned taxis and offices. Edwards had now almost got used to the regular commute between London and Jakarta; at one stage in the last twelve months, he had been spending one week in London and the next week in Jakarta. Then back to London again, to catch up with his other work. But, after several months of this hard regime, fatigue had begun to take hold!

# 4

Edwards had begun to tackle his "Mission Impossible" in a number of ways. As part of the conditions of the proposal that had to be put forward, the "First Daughter's" company had to set up a new, special project company to own and operate the privatised toll road project. A full thirty per cent of the shares in that new company had to be given to the Indonesian government-owned toll road company, which was called Jasa Marga. This company already owned and operated a number of the existing toll roads in Indonesia.

The Princess had assured him, that her company had the funds to subscribe for the rest of the share capital required. But the share capital was only part of the total finance required for this project; the rest would have to be found through loans, and his merchant bank contacts had already told him, that this was impossible. Edwards soon realised that, about three-quarters of the total project costs, would have to be financed by these theoretical loans, that he would have to find.

The remaining one quarter of the total costs, would have to be financed as share capital. Of the total amount of share capital, thirty per cent would have to be given to Jasa Marga. Fortunately, this figure was very close to the amount of aid money that the British Government might well make available to Indonesia, to help cover some of the British goods and services which would be exported, and also to ensure that this project could be won for Britain. Could this aid amount be treated as a contribution so that the share capital that Jasa Marga required could be issued? The project company would acquire assets on one side of its balance sheet from the grant, or "gift", from the British government; this would have to be balanced by a balance sheet liability, being the issuing, free of charge, of the same value of shares in the company to Jasa Marga.

It was a neat "accounting trick", but, could Edwards convince the British government to do this? After all, this project was expanding the policy of privatisation, currently being followed by the British Government, to another country. It would enhance Britain's prestige and trading links, as the British government would be seen to support this Indonesian privatisation policy, by using British aid for this project, in this way.

So Edwards began to talk to his civil service contacts about the project; he already had close links with senior people within various British Government Departments. He was known and trusted; he had once been given a compliment that had greatly reassured him.

"You are considered to be an "honorary civil servant," a senior official at the Department of Trade and Industry had told him. Back behind his desk in London, he smiled to himself as he remembered that remark. A few months after it had been made, he had received a telephone call from the same official. "One of your Directors has written to the Prime Minister about a project," he was told. Edwards had quickly guessed correctly, that it was his Group Director, who had pompously written the letter.

"We know nothing about this project," continued the official. "Could you please find out about it for us, so that we can then write a reply from the Prime Minister?" Wanting to help, Edwards had immediately contacted the Managing Director of the group subsidiary company that he knew would be involved in this project. When he mentioned what had happened, this man laughed with Edwards, about the supercilious action of their Group Director. He then gave Edwards a full description of the project and its current position. Edwards called the senior official back and gave him all this information. "You seem to have learnt a lot about this project in a short time," was the reply. "Could you now please write for me the reply, that I should send back from the Prime Minister?"

Some two weeks later, the Group Director telephoned Edwards. "I have written to the Prime Minister, and I have received a reply from her that I do not like," came the gruff Northern tones, over the telephone line, full of self-importance.

"Send me your letter and the reply," requested Edwards. When copies of the letters arrived on Edwards's desk, the reply from the Prime Minister seemed to be vaguely familiar!

Edwards was, of course, asked to fully justify his request for British Government aid to support his project. First of all, how important was this new toll road to the economy of Java? When asked this question, Edwards always told the same story. He had been driven the current route between Jakarta and Bandung by Roger one Saturday. It had been a hair-raising journey! Even at the weekend, cars, vans and heavy, multi-wheeled trucks were pounding down the current, inadequate road, which had only one lane in each direction. In parts, the road turned into a dirt track, and it also went through the centre of many small towns and villages. Here chickens, dogs and young children, just managed to scamper out of the way of the thundering, polluting, heavy traffic.

In a straight line, it was only some seventy miles between the two cities, but the existing road started off in the wrong direction and then came back to approach Bandung from the south, rather than from the north-west, which would have been more logical. In all, it had taken four-and-a-half hours to reach Bandung. When they had at last arrived, it was time to turn around and start back again for Jakarta. Roger had taken few risks, as trying to overtake had been terrifying, with cars and heavy trucks coming from the opposite direction all the time, on what was a winding road with bend after bend. They took to counting the number of wrecked cars along the road, that, for some reason had not been removed, resulting from the many, probably fatal, accidents that had occurred. "Maybe, they were just left there as a warning to others to drive safely?" thought Edwards wryly.

Edwards had already asked the Managing Director of his group subsidiary company that would build the road, to get his people to come up with a rough estimated total cost. He asked also for this figure to be split up between the goods and services that could be supplied from Britain, and those items that would be supplied locally in Indonesia, such as cement and labour. This company consulted with an engineering design organisation, that specialised in the design of motorways; it first sent a small, expert team to visit the planned route of the new motorway, before coming up with estimates of the materials, equipment and labour that would be needed. This was then incorporated into a full cost estimate, including profit and other outside items.

Taking the estimated total of British content, incorporating materials, equipment and management, that could not be sourced locally, Edwards then applied for export credit, to finance the remaining portion, after the aid money, of this exported British contribution. By then, every leading exporting country had an export credit organisation supported, in one way or another, by its government. These gave loans to help the sale of the country's goods and services exported abroad. Britain was no exception, and Edwards had calculated roughly that, with the combination of this export credit finance and the British aid money, both denominated in British pounds, the British-supplied portion of the project, could be financed.

He succeeded; his civil service colleagues agreed that the British aid money could be treated as a capital injection, from the accounting point of view, and this would be sufficient to provide the share capital that had to be given to Jasa Marga. But the aid money had to be given to the Indonesian-government-owned Jasa Marga first, on the condition that they used it to inject money into the toll road project and received the shareholding they needed from the project company, in return. It was also agreed that the export credit portion could be made available to this privatised toll road project, exceptionally, without any guarantee from the Indonesian government.

This still left three-quarters of the money to find, denominated in Indonesian Rupiah, and representing the major component of materials, expenses and labour that would have to be sourced locally. How could Edwards ever find this money? Loans were required, and he had been told firmly by three leading merchant banks in London, that such loans for this project were impossible. There is often good luck in business, and, fortunately for Edwards, he had just met Peter at a cocktail party, hosted by a leading bank. Peter was undoubtedly a genius; his first degrees had been in Physics, but then he had moved over from Pure Science, to study Economics, and it was in an obscure branch of this Social Science, that he had gained his doctorate.

Peter now worked for a leading Australian bank in the City of London. They met for lunch one day, and Peter had told Edwards about the recent history of the finance package, put together by his bank, for the new privatised road tunnel under Sydney Harbour in Australia. This had been largely financed by a bond issue, with the funding provided by Australian financial institutions in the form of loans. The rate of interest on these bonds was fixed only for the first few years, while the tunnel was being built. It was then increased on a formula based on the amount of traffic using the tunnel and the tolls that this traffic would pay.

This stirred an idea in Edwards's head; could not the same mechanism be used to finance the local content of his Indonesian toll road project? But where would the loans come from? Certainly not from abroad, as Indonesia, with the declining value of its currency and its somewhat uncertain political situation, could not expect to raise overseas loans, for what was really a private sector project. But then it came to him! He remembered being told by one of the British bankers resident in Jakarta, that the Indonesian financial institutions, such as pension funds and insurance companies, had very little to invest in, that gave them a good return for their money.

The large majority of these institutions cash was invested in poorly paying bank deposits; only a tiny part of their funds was placed into shares, as the Indonesian Stock Exchange was very small and the local Government Bond market, gave inferior rates of interest. Could he not somehow devise a bond issue, denominated in Indonesian Rupiah that paid an attractive return to local lenders, linked to the growing income of the toll road? As well as financing the local content of his project, this bond issue could provide a more interesting and much-needed investment medium, in which Indonesian financial institutions could invest their funds.

He discussed his idea with Peter, who was very positive. "It really ticks a number of boxes," he said. "It provides the finance for your project and also provides a valuable, new investment medium for the Indonesian financial institutions. You are developing the Indonesian financial sector towards a new and better direction. I think that a visit to my colleagues in Sydney is necessary for you to discuss this with them. They are the people who put the finance for the new Harbour Tunnel together, and they have the experience to help you with this financing concept." Edwards was excited; he realised that his idea was bringing an element of "financial engineering" to this project.

But why did the major banks not carry out this service for developing economies, such as Indonesia? He thought that the answer was that it went against their established business. They preferred to lend stronger foreign currencies, such as the American dollar, to these countries, even though, when their own local currencies depreciated against the dollar, it became harder for these countries to pay the banks back. These kinds of" financial innovations" could begin to provide alternatives, and work against the future business of the banks.

Edwards quickly coined the phrase "An Indonesian solution for an Indonesian problem" and asked the engineering design organisation to begin a traffic study, to estimate the amount of traffic that would use the new motorway between Jakarta and Bandung. As well as the existing traffic, using the current inadequate road between these two cities, he was told about the concept of "generated traffic". This was the extra traffic that would be created by the new motorway, once it was completed, as a result of it providing an easier journey over a shorter time period. The design firm had expertise in this field too and had already been used to carefully estimate the amount and types of traffic that could be expected to use the Dartford Crossing over the River Thames, once the new privatised suspension bridge there had been completed.

Of course, a toll road in Indonesia was a very different proposition, but, if a conservative view of the situation was taken, it was not beyond the "wit of nan" to come up with some carefully estimated figures that would be accepted by the Indonesian financial institutions. Then, a series of estimates of future toll rates could be made, and, from this combination, a financial projection of the future income of the new toll road could be easily calculated.

# 5

On his next overseas visit for this project, Edwards flew straight to Sydney. There he spent an enjoyable week with the senior staff of the Australian bank that had put together the finance for the new Sydney Harbour Tunnel. They had created an income-linked bond issue, based on the anticipated revenue from the tunnel tolls, for this purpose. The Australians were very open to new ideas, friendly and helpful; they had set up a program of visits for him for the whole week. "I really must find a role for them," Edwards thought!

As well as discussions with the relevant staff of the bank involved with the Harbour Tunnel project, he was taken to a meeting with the Government of New South Wales. They had put the finance, construction and operation of the tunnel out to the private sector to deal with, but would remain a continuing partner in the company that would own the project. As Edwards's company had been involved in the bidding for the new bridge at the Dartford Crossing, he was able to explore some of the principles of privatised projects, with the government officials he met.

He also met with the design team, who showed him an artist's impressions of the completed tunnel project, and with members of the small local company which had been employed to carry out a traffic study and had been engaged, with the bank, in putting together the financial projections for the new Sydney Harbour Tunnel. Some of the income-linked bonds to start off the construction of the tunnel had already been sold to leading Australian financial institutions like pension funds and other investors. The people he met in the bank assured him that they saw no problem with the future tranches of bonds being taken up; there was a high demand for them and the previous amounts issued had been heavily over-subscribed.

Edwards took advantage of his visit; he set aside an evening to attend the Sydney Opera House, of course, at his own expense. It was a real thrill for him to climb the steps and enter this iconic building. The performance that evening was Don Giovanni by Wolfgang Amadeus Mozart. Edwards had attended a live performance of this opera before, but he was pleased to see that the Italian libretto was translated into English, in a rolling format on a long screen above the stage.

Edwards was delighted, too, by his hotel, which was located conveniently close to the financial district. He was used to having the facility of an electric kettle to make tea and coffee in British hotel rooms, but had never found this to be on offer overseas. The Australians had, however, adopted their own method to provide this service. In his room, there was an electric "billycan" provided, along with a supply of tea, coffee, milk and sugar. In the true Australian tradition of the "Jolly Swagman" in the song Waltzing Matilda, Edwards thought to himself, as, before breakfast, he brewed up a cup of tea on his first morning in Sydney!

He took an afternoon off, during the week, to wander around The Rocks, a historic area of narrow lanes in the shadow of Sydney Harbour Bridge. Here had been built some of the oldest buildings in Australia, as this part of the city was very close to the site of Australia's first European settlement in 1788. The Rocks contained some of the oldest pubs in Australia, and, although it had once had a reputation as a slum, it was now an upmarket area for tourists. He bought himself an overpriced, but beautifully painted, boomerang, made in wattle wood from one of the Native Tribal Areas. He also bought a book about the traditional lifestyle of the native Aboriginal peoples.

On his last evening, two of the senior people from the bank, took him across the Sydney Harbour Bridge, to the North Shore. There they had dinner in an excellent fish restaurant, close to the beach. The following morning, he flew out on a Qantas direct flight to Jakarta. Fortunately, it was a day flight and he had a seat by the window. It was a bright, clear day and he watched the lush, green landscape of New South Wales, turn into a scrubby green and then into the reddish-brown of the desert. He was watching this changing panorama when, suddenly, far below, he saw the unmistakable outline of Ayers Rock, the sandstone monolith that marked the centre of Australia. Soon the landscape turned a rich green again, as they flew over the rainforests of North-West Australia. Then they were over the sea and, very soon, the many islands of Indonesia were in sight.

The next day he visited The Princess in her offices. He told her about his visit to Australia. "You must be careful!" she said immediately. "There is currently a dispute between the Government here and Australia. They have tried to lecture us on human rights, and it has not gone down very well." Edwards sat back in his chair; normally he was very politically aware, but he had missed out on the information about this current political dispute. He knew that there had been rumours about continuing repression under the present regime.

The current President Suharto had ousted the first President of Indonesia, Sukarno, in 1967 in a bloody takeover. This had been aimed at destroying the Indonesian Communist Party, with which Sukarno had been, too closely, identified. However, nothing Edwards had seen in Indonesia indicated that the people were repressed; there was a burgeoning economy, and the people he saw seemed hard-working, prosperous and happy under the current regime. Although there was still evidence of poverty, the standard of living for ordinary people seemed to be improving, and the national wealth of Indonesia was increasing from year to year.

Edwards told The Princess about his idea of how an income-indexed local bond issue to finance the toll road, could provide a useful investment medium for the Indonesian pension funds, insurance companies and other financial institutions. She sat back and listened carefully to what he had to say. "You are perfectly right," she said. "I know about this problem as, one of my contacts, is the Chairman of the largest pension fund in Indonesia. It is the Civil Service Pension Fund, and I would like to discuss this idea with him." Edwards readily agreed.

"It is really about the future development of the Indonesian financial sector," he said. "I was told by a banker here, that there was a real shortage of suitable financial opportunities, into which the pension funds and other such institutions, could invest their funds."

Later in the week, he had another meeting with The Princess and some of her colleagues. She looked at him. "I have spoken to my friend," she said. "He tells me that, every month, he gets more money in, taken from the salaries of civil servants, to invest for their future pensions. He has a serious problem, as the types of investments he has available to him, simply do not pay the financial returns he needs, to provide the pensions that he knows he will have to pay out in future years. There is a serious, major mismatch between the income he receives from his current investments and the future liabilities of the pension fund he manages." Edwards was very pleased to receive this confirmation of the major problem that the Indonesian financial sector actually faced, and which he could, perhaps, help, in a small way, to solve.

The next day, Edwards took the short flight to Singapore and then the long non-stop flight back to London. He knew that his desk would be covered with memoranda that would have to be answered and a list of telephone calls, to which he would have to reply. His long-serving and excellent Personal Assistant, Liz, would already have sorted these into higher and lower priorities. She would also have put off any nuisance calls on his time and have organised his diary for the next week with essential meetings only. Appointments for the following weeks would have been put off, until she could speak to him, because he could well be expecting to return to Jakarta again, after just one week of intensive work in London.

Liz had anticipated well; after just two days in the office, a call came through from The Princess in Jakarta. "I want you out here again," she said. "I am arranging for you to meet the Minister of Finance next week." Edwards realised that he would have to tell his Group Director about this very high-level meeting. Otherwise, he would be accused of not keeping him up to date. He called his office and asked to speak to him. "Yes," the booming Northern voice came rudely over the line. Edwards gave him the news. "I must go out there to meet the Minister," was the response. "But I have important meetings here in London early next week. Tell the Minister that I can only meet him on Thursday!"

# 6

So, on that Saturday, Edwards was back on the non-stop Singapore Airways flight to Singapore. By Sunday evening, Jakarta time, he would arrive back in the city that was increasingly becoming his second home. He settled back into his comfortable business class seat. He thought about the Group Director, who would be leaving on next Tuesday night's flight, ready for their meeting with the Minister of Finance on Thursday morning. "Of course, he will not be up here," thought Edwards. "He will be in even greater comfort, at the front of the aircraft, in the first class section." He was so tired from the busy week in the office that he managed, unusually, to get some sleep on the long flight.

Roger had kindly sent him a message that he would meet him at Jakarta Airport, just after the customs channel. It was by now a routine for Edwards: the landing at Changi Airport, the one-hour wait in the Silver Kris Business Lounge and then the short ninety-minute onward flight to Jakarta. As he exited the one-way door from the Indonesian Customs area, there was Roger's smiling face waiting for him.

"Welcome home," he said as he shook his hand. They walked towards the car park. "I have some news for you," Roger said. Edwards waited for it, in anticipation. "The Princess rang me on Thursday. She has arranged for you to meet the Finance Director of the company owned by the President's eldest son. She says that he is probably the best financial brain in Jakarta. She wants you to rehearse the arguments that you will put to the Minister of Finance with him."

"That's fine," replied Edwards. "What day and time am I due to see him?"

"That was the good news," said Roger smiling. "The bad news is that we are going to meet him now at his house."

"But I have just been travelling for 24 hours!" said a desperate Edwards.

"I'm sorry," retorted Roger, "but he flies to Malaysia first thing tomorrow morning, and he is there all week."

In Roger's car, Edwards tried to compose himself for, what he thought, was going to be a difficult meeting. Soon they were driving through a very prosperous suburb of Jakarta. On both sides of the road were luxurious villas, set in large gardens, behind high walls. At last, they pulled up outside an impressive, white residence. They got out of the car and Roger pressed the button on an intercom beside a tall, strong gate. He announced who it was and the gate swung quietly open. They walked through a well-tended garden, to the front door, which was opened for them by a houseboy. They were shown into a large, luxurious living room and offered drinks. Roger chose a cold beer, but Edwards took a strong, black coffee, to wake him up for this unexpected meeting.

The Finance Director entered; he was a young man in his early thirties. He was of mixed race; the obvious result of a union between a local woman and probably a Dutchman. He welcomed Edwards and then sat quietly to hear what he had to say. At the end, he offered a few pieces of advice, then shook Edwards's hand and announced that he was off to bed as he had an early flight in the morning. Edwards climbed sleepily back into Roger's car.

"How did I do?" he asked. "I can't even remember anything that I said."

"You did fine," answered Roger. "You made perfect sense."

That was the last thing Edwards heard; he had immediately fallen deeply asleep, and Roger had difficulty waking him up, when they arrived at the entrance to the Mandarin Oriental Hotel.

When he checked in, there was a message awaiting him from The Princess. Unusually, she did not ask to see him for a business breakfast the following morning. That was what she usually did when he arrived. Instead, she asked him to go to her office at eleven o'clock the following morning. "She must have wanted to give me some extra sleep," thought Edwards wearily, smiling to himself. "She cares about me and knows about the late meeting that I have just attended."

The next morning, he had a late breakfast and walked to the office of The Princess. They greeted each other, as was now usual, with a hug and a kiss on both cheeks. They would, of course, only do this in private, as Indonesia was a Muslim country, although any Islamic influence was very relaxed and liberal. Over the table bearing the welcome strong coffee, The Princess looked at him.

"Why is that man coming?" she asked.

Edwards understood immediately. "Well, he is the Group Director in charge of this project," he replied. "I have to report to him about progress and on important events such as the meeting with the Minister of Finance. He then decided that he would come."

"I have only met him once," said The Princess. "I thought that he was such a rude man. I hope that he behaves himself. How is it, that a man like that, ever reached his position?"

Edwards thought for a moment before he answered. "Well, his father was the Managing Director and part-owner of an engineering company, in the North of England. My group of companies bought that company," he explained. "I think that, as part of the deal, his father insisted that his son be given first a job as the next Managing Director of that company and then a senior position in my group of companies."

They went on to talk about the private meeting that The Princess had attended with the Minister of Finance the previous week. "He very much liked your idea of the income-linked bond issue and how it would help develop the Indonesian financial sector," she said. "But, because my company represents the ruling family and, they might be seen to benefit from it, he asked whether there was some way that you could bring in some kind of participation, from outside Indonesia, for this bond issue? Perhaps an international organisation of some standing would help? But, because this involves the ruling family, you must keep this matter very confidential."

"I understand the politics," replied Edwards. "I will have to think carefully about that. But tell me please, if you can, the answer to one question that has bothered me. How much money will be paid to people, outside your company, to make this project happen?"

The Princess understood immediately what he was asking. How much would have to be paid out in bribes to government officials and others? She smiled at him. "I will be honest with you," she said. "My company is very powerful and we can call in a lot of favours. We have set aside only one million American dollars to pay small amounts out. Mainly this will be spent on some entertaining and some small presents." Edwards nodded; he knew that such a relatively small amount should be acceptable, if he was ever challenged to answer such a question later.

"As we agreed, I have also spoken again to the Chairman of the largest pension fund in Indonesia," said The Princess. "It is the pension fund for the Civil Service, and he confirmed to me that he is very worried because the income that he can make from bank deposits is so small, that he will never be able to meet the value of the pensions he will have to pay out in the future. He will buy the whole of your income-linked bond issue!"

Edwards's mouth fell open. "That is truly amazing!" was all he could say.

The Princess was enjoying herself, showing Edwards how active she had been. "We will meet him on Wednesday, before we meet the Minister of Finance," she said. "Tomorrow I have arranged for you to meet the Managing Director of a leading Indonesian merchant bank.

He has said that he would like to help you to arrange the bond issue on the local market here."

"On Wednesday evening, Roger and I have to meet the Group Director, when he arrives at the airport," said Edwards morosely.

So Roger and Edwards duly reported to the Arrivals Terminal on Wednesday evening. Fortunately, the flight was on time, and Edwards soon spotted the shock of curly red hair. The man was followed by a porter, pushing a trolley laden with a large suitcase.

"Whatever is he bringing that for?" Roger whispered into Edwards's ear. "He is only staying two nights!"

"Maybe he is taking time off here to do a lot of shopping?" Edwards replied thoughtfully.

They escorted the Group Director to Roger's car, and Roger then drove him to his hotel. He had seemed determined not to stay at the same hotel as Edwards; the travel agency, that the London parent company used, had booked him into the Hilton. "He just seems determined to cause trouble," Roger muttered to Edwards, after they had dropped off their largely silent passenger, and Roger was taking Edwards back to his hotel.

"I just hope that he will find his way to the Ministry on time tomorrow morning," was all that Edwards would say.

But Edwards need not have worried; when he arrived at the Ministry the next day, the Group Director was already there, waiting in the Minister's outer office. Soon The Princess arrived, and they were shown in to meet the Minister of Finance, who was accompanied by two of his senior officials. The Group Director slouched back in his chair. He relaxed and opened his legs wide. He let Edwards do all the talking; in fact he said nothing at all, even when he was introduced to the Minister. The Minister was very animated and asked certain pertinent questions. He spoke excellent English; Edwards knew that he had attended the University of California at Berkeley. He and several other Indonesian Ministers, who had attended that same institution, were known in Jakarta as the "Berkeley Mafia!"

Edwards took his time and carefully explained how he hoped that an income-indexed bond issue could be used to finance the Indonesian goods and services, needed to build the new tolled motorway. He explained that he had, fortunately, been able to obtain financial support from the British Government for the goods and services to come from Britain. He voiced his belief that, in a small way, the income-indexed bond issue would help to develop the financial sector in Indonesia. He finally mentioned the positive meeting that The Princess and he had attended, the previous day, with the Chairman of the Civil Service Pension Fund.

"We are setting up a "virtuous circle" to help Indonesia, Minister," Edwards told him. " As well as helping to finance this project, the proposed bond issue will give Indonesian financial institutions an interesting and profitable alternative into which to invest their funds. It will help them, as well, to meet their long-term liabilities to pay out pensions."

The Minister of Finance beamed his approval. "Very good progress," he said. "We certainly appreciate the initiatives that you are taking, and we will offer you our full support."

The meeting over, they left the Minister's office. The Princess turned to the Group Director; she did not mince her words, and her command of English was excellent. "When you meet a Minister of the Indonesian Government," she said to him angrily, "you will show some respect. You should sit upright in your chair, and you should keep your legs together. You do not wave your crotch at everybody in the room!" The man's face turned a bright red and he visibly shrank. Edwards tried to hide his smirk behind his hand, but he needed to be careful. This inadequate but egotistical man could so easily take offence. Indeed, was this perhaps the moment that he decided, even though he had sent Edwards on this "Mission Impossible", to make sure that Edwards would never finally be successful?

# 7

The International Finance Corporation, shortened to the "IFC," is part of the World Bank Group of international financial organisations that are owned by its member governments. Like the World Bank itself, its headquarters are located in Washington D.C. at 2121 Pennsylvania Avenue. The IFC's role is to offer investment, advisory and asset-management services to encourage the advance of the private sector in developing countries.

The IFC's London office was then located on the top floor of an office block at the end of the Haymarket, which leads off Piccadilly Circus. It was headed up by a charming, Austrian economist whom Edwards had met about a year before. On his return to London, with the words of The Princess still in his head about the Minister of Finance's need to bring in some further outside support, Edwards called the IFC's London office. He asked to speak to the charming Austrian. "Hans," he said, "I have recently returned from Indonesia, where I have been working on a major project, and I need to talk to you about it."

The following day, Edwards was in Hans's office, which had an excellent view over London. A few months before, Hans had invited

Edwards and his wife to a buffet lunch, with other guests, to view the Queen's Birthday Parade of Trooping the Colour. The large windows had given an excellent view over Horse Guards Parade, where the ceremony had taken place.

In strict confidence, Edwards told Hans about the privatised toll road project and his now numerous visits to Indonesia. He also explained the support that the British Government was giving and his thinking about a local bond issue, whose income would be linked to the revenue received from the toll road. At the end of his account, Hans looked at him.

"I think that it is an excellent idea," he said, "and one that we should support."

"But how could you do that?" asked Edwards.

"Simply by agreeing to underwrite the bond issue, for a small fee," replied Hans.

Edwards realised immediately that this would satisfy the requirements of the Minister of Finance. "What I would like you to do," asked Hans politely, "is to write me a short paper, not more than two to three pages, summarising what you have just told me. I will then add my recommendation and forward it to the senior levels of the Corporation in Washington."

Over the next few days, Edwards carefully worked and re-worked his description of the Indonesian project. At school, one of his favourite exercises in English had been the writing of a precis; a synopsis, or an outline, of a much longer passage. It had stood him in very good stead, and he found that he could now summarise a fairly complex situation in a matter of a few pages. Only when he was fully satisfied, did he fax the final version to Hans. A few days later, he received back some questions which he managed to answer successfully. It was another few days, before the formal response arrived; "his proposal would now be considered by the IFC Board of Directors."

Meanwhile, a message had been received from The Princess: it would be good if a full presentation could be made, at a one-day conference that she would set up, about the proposed bond issue, the income of which would be linked to the revenues of the toll road. The audience would be drawn from a mix of senior government officials and senior representatives of Indonesian pension funds, banks and insurance companies. For a moment, this threw Edwards into some confusion; how could he alone keep such a conference educated and entertained for a whole day? Then, fortunately, he remembered his new-found Australian friends. He contacted them and they appeared willing to help.

During his next visit to Jakarta, the one-day conference had been arranged. A team of three people, from the bank in Sydney, flew in to help Edwards. On the day, Edwards delivered the introduction to the packed audience and then left it to the bankers to make their individual presentations. There was a buffet lunch provided and, at the end of the day, Edwards summed up the proceedings.

"I think a very successful day," said The Princess and went on to thank the Australians for coming. "You may have done something to help repair the relations between our two governments," she said to them.

"That was partly our intention," replied the senior Australian. "But we would also like to do more business here."

"I will introduce you to my friend who runs the top Indonesian merchant bank," said The Princess. "I am sure that you can work together, with them, to make this bond issue a success. From the initial views that I have been able to gather today, there are now many Indonesian institutions that would like to take part of this bond issue. These are in addition to the Civil Service Pension Fund, which has already said, that it would like to take it all. We will have to share it out between all these financial institutions carefully."

The next day, Edwards met The Princess, privately and briefed her on the progress that he had made with the IFC. She expressed her strong approval.

Back in London, Edwards was informed by a civil servant, that he knew, at the Government organisation for the British aid budget, that his responsible Minister would be leaving for a two-week visit to South East Asia the following month. The Minister would be visiting Indonesia, and he would meet with his opposite number there. Would Edwards like to prepare a brief for the Minister on the toll road project, so that he could talk about it? Edwards willingly prepared the brief, and then sent it to his civil service colleague. But what should he do about the Indonesian side? Edwards decided to send his brief also to The Princess, and explain about the forthcoming British Ministerial visit.

The civil servant had accompanied his Minister on the overseas visit; as soon as he got back, he telephoned Edwards. "I don't know how you did it," he said, "but my Minister and theirs were competing against each other to mention your project first! It all went very well. It has proved not only to be a major talking point between them, but it has also cemented a renewal of good diplomatic relations between Britain and Indonesia. My Minister is very pleased."

But now a potential difficulty appeared; the design company, appointed to design the new road and to come up with some financial projections of its future toll income, had been complaining. They felt that they were being asked to do too much work without being paid, and without being certain, that this project would ever happen. Edwards met with the Managing Director of the design company and some of the Directors of his construction company, who would actually build the road. A compromise was reached; Edwards would try and get some advance payment from the British aid budget, that had already been allocated, to support this project.

Edwards was then involved in a series of meetings with the senior British Government officials, all of whom he knew well. They came from the Foreign Office, the Department of Trade and Industry, the Export Credit Agency and the Overseas Development Administration, that then oversaw the British aid budget. The discussions revolved around the need to keep this project one that Britain could win, particularly following the recent successful Ministerial visit to Indonesia. Eventually, it was agreed that, exceptionally, a sufficient amount of the aid budget allocated for this project, could be advanced to the design company, against their proven work on this project, and up to an agreed total amount.

"Another problem solved," thought Edwards, as he went about his normal work dealing with other projects and the demands for help from the Marketing Departments of the various operating companies, in his group. They all seemed to be trying to sell to an increasing number of countries. Again and again, he had to reject projects that they had identified, but, for which, there was no chance of raising the required finance. Although he tried his best to teach them the principles of sound finance and what to look for, he was still sometimes surprised. One day, a Marketing Manager called him and demanded a finance package for the project he was working on.

"When do you need this by?" asked Edwards.

"By tomorrow, please!" was the reply. "The proposal has to go in by then."

"I suppose that you have given the same notice, to the company who has to do the design for the building?" asked Edwards.

"Of course not," came the reply. "They need more time to do it than that!"

"You must understand that a finance package takes as much time to put together as designing the building," said Edwards calmly, although he did not feel very calm inside!

# 8

A few days later, he received a telephone call from Hans. "Your proposal has been approved by the IFC Board of Directors," he said, "but subject to you, and a Director from your parent company, visiting Washington and meeting with a team from the IFC. They have some questions to ask you. Their team will be led by the third most-senior person in the organisation." As much as he did not want to, Edwards knew that he would have to invite the Group Director to Washington for this meeting. He called his secretary to arrange an appointment. It was with some trepidation that he left his office, on the appointed day, to meet this man.

This time, he was given more attention; he explained carefully why the IFC needed to be involved in the project and why it was necessary for them both to visit Washington. "I don't think that it is necessary," came the immediate reply. Patiently, Edwards explained the reason again; why he had brought the IFC into this transaction. The

Indonesian Minister of Finance had privately requested that an outside organisation, such as this, should be brought in, and the IFC had the undoubted status, to fulfil this role. The Group Director was, as always, disagreeable: he tried to bully Edwards, saying that he had not handled the transaction properly. But Edwards refused to be bullied by him. Eventually and grudgingly, the Group Director agreed to travel to Washington for the meeting.

So a date was set and agreed by all parties for the meeting in Washington. Edwards decided to travel out on a day flight the day before and have a good night's sleep before this important event. He received a call from the Group Director: "I am very busy that week. I will have to fly out on Concorde that morning, but the travel agency has booked me onto an inconvenient onward flight from New York."

By now, Edwards knew the airline timetables very well. "I think that you will find," he said, "that one hour after the Concorde flight they have booked you on to New York, there is a direct Concorde flight from Heathrow to Washington."

"I will bloody kill them!" was the only reply he received.

So Edwards flew out on his comfortable daylight flight and stayed at a convenient, but inexpensive hotel, that was only a few minutes' walk from the IFC building. It was an old hotel and, when he checked in, he was surprised to find that he had been upgraded to a small suite of rooms. It had been arranged that the Group Director would collect him from his hotel, once he had landed on Concorde and had arrived in the city. About one hour before the IFC meeting was due to happen, there was a rapid knocking on Edwards's door. The Group Director strode in and looked around the suite. Unusually, a smile came over his face. "Big enough for a bloody party!" was his only comment.

They walked together to the IFC building and were shown up to a Meeting Room on the top floor. There they were received by the senior IFC man and two of his assistants. For over two hours they carefully questioned Edwards; the Group Director made absolutely no contribution to the meeting. "At least he is sitting up and paying attention!" thought Edwards. The expected question came up about the amount of money that would be paid to outside parties, by the Indonesian company, to make the project happen. Edwards was fully aware of the IFC's view on excessive corruption and he answered the question honestly, with what he had been told by The Princess. The senior IFC man seemed satisfied with his answer; at the end, he shook Edwards firmly by the hand. "We will let you know our final decision in a few days' time," he said.

Edwards and the Group Director descended in the lift to the ground floor and then out of the building onto the pavement of Pennsylvania Avenue. The Group Director turned to Edwards. "I am not going to deal with those people!" he growled.

Edwards was nonplussed; "But the meeting went very well!" he said. "I am sure that they will give their final approval, in a few days, to underwrite the bond issue for the toll road project."

But the Group Director was having none of it; when asked by Edwards what was the reason he did not want to deal with the IFC, he could give none. He just stamped his foot and repeated that "he did not want those people involved with the project." Edwards tried to argue with him but to no avail. The Group Director now seemed determined, for some reason, to stop Edwards putting into place, probably, the last piece he needed, to complete a successful financing for this toll road project. They found a taxi to the airport and then took the overnight flight back to London.

All the way, the man was uncommunicative; he refused to listen to any of Edwards's arguments. As he was flying with a Group Director, Edwards was entitled to a first class seat, to sit next to him. They boarded the aircraft; rudely the Group Director refused any attention from the charming flight attendants. Instead, he took a blanket and, wrapping his head in it, went instantly to sleep. At least Edwards could enjoy the first class treatment and the excellent dinner that was served.

Beside him, the Group Director snored loudly; Edwards could not sleep as his mind was in turmoil. Why had the Group Director refused to deal with the IFC, when they provided the final, vital part to finance the toll road project? The man did not even bother with breakfast, but awoke just as they were beginning to land at Heathrow Airport. He turned to Edwards; "I have the corporate helicopter waiting to meet me," he said. "Can I drop you anywhere?" Edwards, who lived a relatively short taxi ride from Heathrow, declined the offer.

Back in his office, Edwards sat and thought about what he could do? He felt an idiot having to tell The Princess that they would not now use the services and support of the IFC. This organisation fitted in, so well, with the private request from the Minister of Finance, to use an international organisation to support the project. In the end, he decided to talk the situation over, in strict confidence, with a senior official from the British Government who he knew well; after all, they were already substantially supporting this project. "I have always thought it," said the official. "That man is mad, and I will tell him so to his face. I might even be able to get my Minister to tell him also."

Internally, Edwards decided on an appeal to the man to whom he now also partly reported; the Group Treasurer had only recently been appointed, but Edwards had met with him and respected his new colleague. He asked for a meeting and reported to him what had happened. The man was aghast; "He just does not seem to be thinking sensibly," was his response. "I will approach the Group Managing Director and register my concern. I will try and get this decision reversed." But it was to no avail: the Group Managing Director decided to support the decision of the Group Director, not to use the IFC to underwrite the income-indexed bond issue for the Indonesian toll road project.

So Edwards then had to tell Hans that they would not be using the IFC. As usual, the man was charming; "Perhaps next time," he said. Edwards now had to screw up his courage and communicate this bad news to The Princess. She was not at all pleased. On the telephone line from Jakarta, she asked him the reason. He was, as always, honest with her. "It was the Group Director who made this decision," he said.

"I thought so," she replied. "I never did like that man! I am afraid that this could well change the situation for your company. We will have to reconsider the whole matter. I will try to let you know, as soon as I can, what decision we have made."

But Edwards did not see or hear back from her again. The traffic study, financed by British taxpayer's money, was completed and a copy was given to the Indonesians. But Edwards had been told that he could no longer visit Jakarta and that his work on this project was no longer needed. With no direction from him, the project began to flounder. Some months later, he heard that the Group Director had appointed a leading merchant bank in Hong Kong to come up with a major study and a solution for the financing of the Indonesian toll road project. In all, a total of ten million pounds would be paid in fees to this bank, for this task, and this money would also be provided by the British Government, by way of an aid grant!

It soon became clear why this had happened; the Group Director left Britain to live in Hong Kong. He continued to work for Edwards's company for a while and then left to set up his own business. Some months later, Edwards met with the senior civil servant, who had been the main person who had helped him get the support of the British Government for the Indonesian toll road project. They discussed the Group Director and what had happened with the project.

"You know that the Managing Director of that merchant bank in Hong Kong is a close personal friend of his?" commented the official. "I have heard that he has now made your Group Director a Consultant to the bank. I wonder if he received a hidden commission for giving them that study to do?"

Edwards gasped; he had not thought of that possibility. "I cannot believe that" he replied. "I thought that it was just that he was really jealous of me, for getting so close, to a successful innovative financing."

"Don't worry," continued the senior official, "we will get him in the end. He has wasted a lot of British taxpayer's money by not going along with what you had planned. I have heard that the Inland Revenue is now looking very carefully into his private tax affairs here and, that they are already not very happy, with what they have found!"

# 9

Time went by; the group that Edwards worked for was beginning to suffer financial problems. They seemed to have indulged in some "creative accounting"; taking profits from their various construction contracts, before they had been really earned by them! The group's next set of annual accounts were "qualified" by their independent accountants or auditors. That is, they said that they could not really accept the figures that they had been given. The price of the group's shares on the London Stock Exchange nose-dived! The effort to find new business slowed, and Edwards's visits overseas to try and find finance for various projects ceased.

It therefore came as no surprise when, one day, Edwards was called in to meet the group's Finance Director. "I am sorry to tell you," he said, "that we have decided to close down all our international business and, I am afraid, we will have to make you and your team redundant. We will, of course, pay you six month's salary and other compensation, but that is what must happen."

So Edwards had to find a new job. An old friend arranged for him to have dinner with the Chairman of the engineering design organisation that had designed the Indonesian toll road and carried out the traffic survey for this project. He was offered a six-month assignment to help them with some of their financing problems with the various other international projects that they were working on. That was then extended, by their Managing Director, for another two-year period, on a part-time basis.

One morning at home, Edwards received a telephone call. It was a senior Government official whom he knew well.

"Are you still looking for a permanent position?" he was asked.

"Yes," replied Edwards.

"There is a position coming up in a Government organisation which promotes British exports," his friend went on. "I suggest that you apply for it. I will give you the name and address of the man you should write to. He is expecting your letter."

So Edwards wrote his letter and heard back that his application was being considered. He was then called for an interview with the relevant senior civil servant. "I have to mention that we are interviewing two other candidates," he was told, "but we will get back to you with a decision as soon as possible." The following morning, Edwards' telephone at home rang again; it was the same senior official who had interviewed him. "I am happy to tell you that you are to be offered the position with us," he said.

After Edwards had signed a contract and had been put through the process of security clearance, he started his new job. He enjoyed working with the civil servants in the organisation; they were not what he had expected. They were all talented, educated people who were highly motivated and worked very hard on what they were doing. "I will never criticise civil servants again," he thought. He was allowed to carry on with his outside consultancy to the design engineering company, as long as it presented no conflict of interest. One morning, he received a call from its Managing Director.

"We would like you to come along for a meeting next week," he was told. "We are going to consider the results of the new study on the Indonesian toll road project; that is the one that the merchant bank in Hong Kong has carried out."

"I would very much like to see a copy of their study first," was Edwards's response. So that evening, he collected the three thick volumes of the study from the design company's offices. "I suppose that you have to have three thick volumes, to justify a fee of ten million pounds," he thought to himself.

In his spare time over the next week, he read through the three volumes. He read first the conclusions, and then read back to any section that he wanted further clarification about. The merchant bank had taken the British aid amount and the export credit to cover the British pound portion of the contract, just as Edwards had negotiated it. But for the local content of the contract, they proposed four different solutions. They suggested a much reduced income-linked bond issue in the local Indonesian currency. For the rest of the money required, they followed what was in their own interests; a large American dollar loan, although American dollars were not even needed for this project! Then they suggested two American dollar bond issues; one ranking in security of repayment better than the other. Using these arrangements, it was clear that the merchant bank could be sure of receiving large fees and attractive banking business. "Just a waste of ten million pounds of British taxpayer's money!" thought Edwards, as he concluded his detailed examination of this expensive study.

When the appointed day came, he was shown into the top-floor Board Room of the engineering design company, where the Managing Director and his other Directors were awaiting his verdict. "I have read through all this very carefully," said Edwards, indicating the three thick volumes on the table in front of him. "I always believe in keeping things as simple as possible. My view is that their plan will not work. They have made the financing package far too complex. They are seeking funds from at least six different sources in six very different ways. My aim was always to keep the financing from just a limited number of sources to try and ensure success. Now they are suggesting something that is so complicated, that the odds of it actually happening, are close to zero!"

He was asked some questions which he responded to. At the end of the meeting, the Managing Director turned to him. "I have to agree with you," he said. "They seem to have made their solution very complicated. Perhaps, they did that, to justify their large fee? Fortunately, we have come out of all of this very well. All our work has been paid for by the British taxpayer."

Edwards's prediction was correct. The complex financing, suggested by the Hong Kong merchant bank, never took place. Instead, the Indonesians found their own solution and Edwards's former employers were not part of it. Working quietly with the Australian bank, that Edwards had introduced, the Indonesians financed the toll road themselves. No British goods or services were imported; everything that was needed to build the toll road was found within Indonesia.

A local Indonesian bond issue, with its income linked to the revenue of the toll road, to start once construction was completed, was launched in Indonesia. The issue was led by the Indonesian merchant bank that Edwards had met, advised by the Australian bank, and within hours, the hungry Indonesian institutions had subscribed for it all. The same method was then used again, many times over, by Jasa Marga, to fund subsequent toll roads throughout the country. So the ideas that Edwards had produced, and all the work that he had done, was not completely wasted!

Edwards did not hear from The Princess again. In 1998, after thirty years in office, President Suharto finally handed over to his Vice President, on a temporary basis, and then democratic elections for a new President were held. Edwards did not forget his visits to Jakarta which, for a time, had almost become his second home. He later heard a true story, from one of his reliable contacts there. He did not know what to make of it. Had The Princess made some real enemies, or was it just a warning to her to keep silent, about what she had learnt while she had been working for the daughter of the President?

A few years before President Suharto had left office, The Princess had, at last, got married. She married a local Indonesian film actor, and on the first night of their honeymoon, they had stayed in a very luxurious "boutique hotel" in Jakarta. In the middle of the night, a sniper's bullet had come through their bedroom window, and buried itself deep within the mattress of the double bed, on which they were sleeping! Fortunately, neither The Princess, nor her new husband, had been harmed.

THE END

# Tradecraft

-

*"When you leave Africa, as the plane lifts, you feel that more than leaving a continent, you are leaving a state of mind."*

— **Francesca Marciano**

# 1

Edwards was wondering from which direction the bullet would come! For some reason, he felt that his life was at risk. As directed, he was standing by the red rubbish bin and he made a perfect target. The bin was in the middle of a car park, next to a shopping centre, in one of this city's suburbs. It was the middle of the day and the car park was, at best, a quarter full. There was absolutely nobody around and Edwards was beginning to feel very exposed.

He knew that, in this country, human life was very cheap. People could be hired, for the equivalent of less than one hundred pounds, to kill a man, and all kinds of guns were freely available. The African sun beat down but, given the altitude of this city, it was not hot. A gusting wind blew brushwood around the car park and, even though he wore glasses, Edwards could feel the dust and the grit getting into his eyes.

The morning had started off well, with a good breakfast in his five-star hotel. The hotel was in the new financial centre that had been built up, over the recent years, in what had once been, one of the city's suburbs. The aim was for banks and companies to escape from the old, run-down city centre which was now partly boarded up and half empty. It had been largely taken over by the poor, black population. The new financial centre was full of gleaming, new, glass skyscrapers for multi-office use, boutiques, bars, hotels and coffee shops. It was considered to be one of the few safe places where one could walk around freely, in this city.

Back in London, Edwards had been given the required security briefing. He had been told that, on arriving at the airport, he should not go to the taxi rank for his car into the centre of the city. Instead, he should go to the Information Desk in the airport concourse and ask for a car to be called. They would know which taxi firm to call, and Edwards was to wait there, until a driver arrived and identified himself to the people behind the desk.

His long-standing friend in London, who had been born here, but had spent many years in England, had been very clear. "You will find that Hendriks will be very suspicious," he had said. "But it is well worth your while to talk to him as he knows very well what is really happening in the country. He is an investigative journalist and he also helps certain, very carefully selected companies to understand his country. But he has been very critical of the government and his life may be at risk." His friend had sent a message to Hendriks that Edwards would be visiting the city and to expect his call.

The previous day, Edwards had called the telephone number his friend had given him. Edwards had spoken to his secretary, as Hendriks himself was out of the office, and a meeting with him had been arranged for the following morning. Edwards had made a careful note of the office address, where the meeting was to take place, and had given it to the taxi driver that had been hailed by the hotel doorman that morning. Edwards had assumed, therefore, that this driver could be trusted. The taxi had deposited Edwards at a low building in a long broad road, with three lanes of traffic going in either direction. He was pleased that he was a few minutes early, as he entered the front door.

The office he wanted was on the ground floor, to the left of the entrance door. There was a pretty, blonde girl sitting behind a desk. "Good morning. I am Mr. Edwards to see Mr. Hendriks," Edwards said. She smiled at him and then asked to see his British passport, which, fortunately, Edwards always carried with him. Having satisfied herself that he was indeed "Mr. Edwards," she said that, unfortunately, Mr. Hendriks was out of the office, but would meet Mr. Edwards at another address. She had already called a car to take him there and it would arrive in a few minutes. The car would, of course, be paid for by them, and it belonged to a taxi firm that they used all the time. Edwards saw nothing suspicious in this and sat down to wait for the expected vehicle.

They had been driving for about five minutes when his mobile telephone rang; the caller identified himself as Hendriks. "There is a change of plan," he said and asked Edwards if he had a piece of paper and pen to take down the new address where they were to meet. Edwards carefully noted it down and then repeated it back to Hendriks, just to be sure. He then passed the piece of paper to the driver and asked him to go to that new address. The driver looked at him strangely, but made a rapid U-turn and they went off in the opposite direction.

 Five minutes later, Edwards's mobile telephone rang again. It was Hendriks with another change of plan. This time he gave Edwards the name of a shopping centre in a suburb of the city and told him to ask the driver to drop him at Entrance Number 3. "Straight in front of you, there is a red rubbish bin," said Hendriks. "I will meet you by that bin, if you would kindly wait for me there." This time the driver cursed under his breath, when Edwards handed him the new destination that he had noted down. He made a vicious turn at the next intersection and they were again heading off in a completely different direction.

# 2

In the middle of the nearly empty car park, Edwards tried to remember how he had ever got there. Some six months before, he had been asked to attend a conference about doing business with the country he was now in. It had been a two-day affair in Edinburgh, and, rather than face a long train journey, he had flown up to Scotland from Heathrow Airport, which was only forty minutes by taxi from Edwards's home. It was the late 1990s, and Edwards now worked for a government-sponsored organisation to help promote British exports. He handled both some of the marketing and the financial aspects of prospective major deals, involving mainly large British companies. In Edinburgh, he had stayed in a first-class hotel, whose main decoration, for carpets and furnishings, was its own tartan. After a while, this had begun to grate with Edwards, but the hotel was very comfortable and the food was good.

The conference was held in the city's Conference Centre, a short walk away. It was at the formal dinner, on the last evening, when it was suggested to Edwards, that he should sit next to one of the African delegates. The suggestion had come from a senior Director, who worked for a major British company and whom Edwards knew well. "I am sure that you will find him interesting," said the Director and then, whispering into Edwards's ear, he explained who this man was, and who this man's brothers were.

Edwards did what he was asked; he sat down next to this delegate, introduced himself and described his role. The man was not an African; his skin was brown and he had piercing dark eyes. Edwards was later to learn that he was of Middle Eastern origin, but his parents had moved to Africa before he was born. Later, this man had claimed to Edwards to have been part of the "liberation struggle" against the white oppressors of his country, and that he had been captured and tortured by the Secret Police of the former regime. They had tortured him so badly, that he could no longer father any children.

After dinner, he introduced Edwards to a number of Government Ministers and to some senior Government officials, who were also visiting Edinburgh to promote their country. It was clear to Edwards, that, his new contact was held in great respect by all of them. Much more was to follow; Edwards had now travelled out to this country, several times, to meet this man, whom he had now nicknamed "The Sheikh" because of his Arab background. He had also met him, a number of times, when he had visited London. But Edwards had begun to hear certain rumours about him, and this explained his call to his old friend, in London, for help. This had resulted in the meeting now planned with Hendriks.

Suddenly, Hendriks touched his arm; Edwards had not seen him as he had cleverly approached him from the side. Hendriks held his forefinger up to his lips to indicate silence, and then beckoned Edwards to follow him. He led Edwards to his car and unlocked it; only then did Edwards realise that Hendriks had been keeping him under observation, from his car, to make sure that nobody had followed Edwards. This also explained the several changes in destination that Hendriks had made; it was to confuse any followers. Hendriks took out what seemed to be his mobile telephone from the car's glove compartment, and silently indicated to Edwards, that he would like to have Edwards's mobile telephone handed to him. He then placed both mobile telephones in the glove compartment, locked his car and motioned for Edwards to follow him.

Edwards was very pleased with the caution that Hendriks was showing. The most efficient surveillance tool, that any government can now have, is the mobile telephone. If the government has the right technology, it can not only track the owner's movements and listen to all the mobile telephone calls made by them, but also, using the phone's microphone, listen-in to any face-to-face conversations that are taking place in the mobile telephone's vicinity. Turning the telephone off does not help, as the technology can activate the mobile telephone, without the owner even realising that it is on and broadcasting to the Government listeners. Before he left London, Edwards had been warned that, the government of this country where he now was, had already bought such advanced surveillance technology and was using it widely.

They entered the shopping centre. Just inside the door was a park bench, which would not have been out of place in any English park. Beside the bench was an artificial waterfall, producing a continuous flow of "white sound." This would protect them, against any directional microphones being used, to try to hear their conversation. "Sit down," said Hendriks, speaking for the first time. "We can talk here safely." They talked for nearly two hours before Edwards had understood enough. Then they walked back to Hendriks's car, where he returned Edwards's mobile telephone. Hendriks then used his own mobile telephone to call the taxi firm that he used, to order a car to take Edwards back to his hotel.

# 3

This country was not Edwards's only experience of Africa. He had visited several African countries, including a memorable visit to Nigeria, his first trip to Africa, which had taken place just under twenty years before. Edwards well remembered this visit; he had landed very early in the morning at Lagos International Airport, on the British Caledonian Airways aircraft, with its smart internal tartan decoration. From his comfortable business class seat, he had surveyed the deeply dark African night outside. As he got off the air-conditioned aircraft, the heat and humidity had hit him like a wall!

He managed to slowly negotiate the crowded, noisy confusion of the Arrivals Hall. Once through Arrivals, their "local man," who lived in Lagos, and worked for the same British international construction group that Edwards then worked for, was there to meet him. After greeting Edwards, he had led him to the car park and the comfortable, air-conditioned car with an African driver, which was to take Edwards to the Domestic Airport for his short onward flight to the city of Enugu in Eastern Nigeria. There his company was involved in a potential major construction project, and Edwards was to join some of his colleagues, who were already staying there.

Lagos Domestic Airport is close to the International Airport, but such were the badly planned and maintained roads, that the journey between the two, could take more than an hour. Edwards chatted to their "local man," who sat with him on the back seat of the car. But during their conversation, he also looked out of the car window. He had never seen such a deep darkness; the moon and stars were obscured by heavy clouds. There were no lights showing anywhere until, suddenly, there were several waving torches ahead. The driver screeched to a halt and wound down his window. The muzzle of a sub-machine gun was pushed through the car window and pointed directly at the driver.

In the darkness outside, Edwards could see the sinister outline of several heavily armed men. "It's the Army," hissed the "local man" into Edwards's ear. "Keep very quiet and give me your passport."

"Open the boot!" came the curt order to the driver, who, Edwards thought, replied very wisely with a quick "Yes, sir!"

The driver got out to open the boot, and the soldiers poked around in it. Finding nothing of interest, they turned their attention to the two white passengers on the back seat. The "local man" wound down his window and spoke politely to the soldiers, as he handed over the two British passports. Torches were shone into their faces, to make sure that they looked like their passport photographs. With the passports handed back, they were waved on. Edwards relaxed, "That wasn't so bad," he said.

"They were on good behaviour tonight," said the "local man," smiling to himself. "When they have been drinking, they turn into the bad guys and take all your money and valuables."

They arrived at Lagos Domestic Airport and the "local man" gave Edwards his last piece of advice. "When you leave Nigeria," he said, "transfer all of your British money out of your wallet and leave a small amount of the local currency in it. At the airport, after you pass through security, you will be asked for your wallet. They will confiscate all the local currency, as you are not allowed to take it out of the country. If there is any British money in your wallet, they will take that as well. If you protest, you will never leave the country!" Edwards thanked him, shook hands and got out of the car.

He entered the Domestic Airport Terminal; if the International Terminal was full of noise and confusion, this Terminal was in total chaos. The air-conditioning did not work, people were sleeping all over the floor and the unpleasant smells filling the air were unbelievable. None of the television monitors, needed to give details of arrivals and departures, were working. The only announcements were in English, but in such a deep Nigerian accent, that Edwards could hardly understand anything that was said. He could see no manned desk, where he could exchange his ticket, for a boarding card for his onward flight.

Edwards grabbed a seat that had just been vacated by a large, black lady, and gazed around morosely. Normally, he would have spent his time in the business class lounge, but, domestically, Nigerian Airways was a one-class airline and no such, more pleasant, facilities were available. He wanted a drink, but he did not dare to drink anything except from a sealed bottle. He wanted to use the lavatory, before boarding his local flight, but the stench from the toilets was so overpowering, that he did not even dare to approach them. His flight was timed to leave at ten o'clock, so all he could do was to wait and hope for the best.

At these kinds of moments, Edwards remembered the quote from the late, patrician Prime Minister Harold Macmillan, who once said, "Exporting is fun!" In 1945, Sir Stafford Cripps, who had just been appointed President of the Board of Trade, had used the phrase "Export or Die." "More appropriate," mused Edwards, as he looked out of the window.

Outside, the sun had risen and the weather had changed rapidly. The clouds were gone and the temperature and humidity seemed to have begun to fall. A gusting wind had come up, which seemed full of dust, and that at times obscured the visibility. Edwards had heard about the Harmattan wind, which, at this time of the year, could blow from the Sahara Desert. It could be full of sand particles, and it could affect the whole of West Africa, for days on end.

At about ten-thirty, the loudspeaker system came to life. There was a series of announcements, in a deep Nigerian accent. Edwards just caught the name "Enugu" and stood up. Several flights seemed to have been called together, as most of the people in the Terminal, were now surging forward and trying to get through one fairly narrow door. Edwards joined them in a great crush of sweating bodies and eventually, managed to squeeze outside. In the distance, there were six Nigerian Airways aircraft parked in a line on the tarmac, and people were running to board their aircraft. Edwards joined them, jogging along gripping his "carry-on" luggage, that contained all his needs.

There was no indication to Edwards which aircraft he was supposed to board. He spied a group of airport workers, laughing and joking together. He approached the one who seemed to be the oldest and asked him which aircraft was for Enugu. He thought that the man said "fourth", but, just to be sure, Edwards held up four fingers and asked if this was right. The man nodded and smiled at the poor white man who, obviously, was completely out of his depth in an airport environment.

Thankfully, Edwards climbed the ladder onto the fourth jet aircraft in the line; he sincerely hoped that he was on the right aeroplane. The passenger seats inside were torn and dirty but, since there were only a few passengers, Edwards was able to select one, in a reasonable state of repair. Nobody asked him to show a boarding card or a ticket; he could have flown free of charge. The door was shut by the sole cabin attendant and the engines started; there was no "Safety Announcement." Having carried out this single duty, the cabin attendant sat at the front of the aircraft and paid absolutely no attention to the passengers for the whole of the flight.

The plane shot down the runway; as it took off, the door to the flight deck swung open. Inside the flight deck, there was one huge black pilot. He was so large that he covered both the pilot and co-pilot seats.

After about an hour into the flight, Edwards sensed that the plane was beginning to descend for its landing at Enugu. Edwards looked out of the window. Below he could see nothing of the ground. The Harmattan wind was now blowing strongly and the air was full of sand from the Sahara Desert. Lower and lower the plane descended, but still no sign of land appeared. Edwards thought to himself, "I very much doubt that they have any landing aids, or even a radar set which works, at Enugu Airport."

Their descent continued; he looked again out of the window. There was still absolutely no sign of the land below! Everything had been obscured by the windborne sand. He prepared himself wistfully for death. "It may happen now," he thought. "I have had a good and interesting life, and, if it is going to end here, then so be it." At the front, the huge pilot seemed totally absorbed in the controls. Suddenly, there was the slightest of bumps and they had landed on the runway! "That guy is a brilliant pilot," thought Edwards. "That is the softest landing that I have ever had."

One week later, he was back in London. The following day, he read in a newspaper, that exactly the same flight, on the same day of the week and at the same time, had crashed into a hill, while trying to land at Enugu. Most of the people on board had been killed!

# 4

Back in his hotel room, Edwards decided to make some notes of his conversation with Hendriks. He got out a notebook and scribbled down what he remembered of their discussion. Fortunately, Edwards's handwriting was hardly decipherable to any normal person. Nevertheless, after he had finished his notes, Edwards locked the notebook into his briefcase. He knew that anyone with the right lock-picking tools could easily open his briefcase. Breakfast was now a long time ago and he was feeling very hungry.

 He did not want to take his briefcase down to the hotel dining room, so he arranged his briefcase at the slightest angle under the bedroom desk. Anyone picking up the briefcase, would probably put it back exactly straight and he would know, when he returned to his room, that it had been tampered with. He added an extra flourish, which he had once seen Sean Connery carry out in a James Bond film. He pulled one single hair out of his scalp, moistened it and laid it across the opening of the briefcase. Anyone opening his briefcase, would probably displace the hair, without noticing it.

Down in the plush dining room, Edwards indulged himself in a large steak and chips, complemented by a bottle of good red wine, to calm his nerves after that morning's clandestine meeting. The hotel he was staying in was very luxurious and catered for all his needs. But his mind drifted back to other hotels he had stayed in around the world. Probably the worst ever had been the President Hotel in Enugu in Eastern Nigeria. The Biafran War, fought and lost for the independence of Eastern Nigeria, had finished over ten years before. But Enugu, which had been the capital of that short-lived state, was still, in many ways, a defeated and deprived city.

From the outside, the President Hotel looked a suitable place to stay and displayed its "4 Star" status over its main entrance. But inside, there were faded carpets and curtains and broken-down furniture. The water supply was limited to only one hour a day, and during that hour, guests were expected to fill their own large calabash, which stood in their en-suite bathroom. On registering, each guest would be handed a bath plug for their bath, and would be expected to return it, when checking out. This would enable them to have a cold bath each morning, using the long-handled ladle, which was also provided at Reception, for each guest, to slowly fill their bath from the calabash.

Edwards quickly learnt to place his shoes by his bed at night and shake them out very carefully, before putting them on in the morning. As he stepped away from the bed, numerous small creatures fled to the corners of his room or under the skirting board, only to reappear during the hours of darkness. Breakfast was just as entertaining; the only things that he felt were safe to eat, were boiled eggs and some plain bread. Fortunately, the coffee was served very hot and therefore, he deemed, reasonably safe to drink. All the milk came out of a tin-can, which you collected from a table, and then opened yourself, using the tin opener provided. The tin opener was tied, by a piece of string, to one of the table legs, to prevent theft!

Although Christmas was still over a month away, the hotel staff, who were all Christians in this part of Nigeria, had erected a poorly decorated Christmas tree in the dining room, complete with flashing coloured lights. There was also a sound system, which played Christmas carols. The only problem was that the system was faulty, and the Christmas carols were played at a slowed-down speed!

Despite all this, Edwards had admired the local Igbo people. They were always beautifully dressed and both sexes, were tall, statuesque and handsome. They were always smiling and only too willing to help in any way they could. The exception to this seemed to be the President Hotel's telex operator. In those days, the telex was about the only way to communicate with London, as the telephone system, in this part of Nigeria, was totally unreliable. The hotel had a Telex Room, with an antiquated telex machine, and an inadequate operator who, after two days, had still not been able to send a short but urgent telex message from Edwards to his company in London.

Edwards had learnt to operate a telex machine, during one of his previous jobs working in the financial sector in the City of London. He decided, in desperation, to give the official hotel telex operator some money, so that he could get access to the hotel's Telex Room, after he had left for the day. During that evening and through the night, he tried to send the urgent telex message himself out to London. At two o'clock the following morning, he eventually managed to send the message, and the next day a reply was safely received.

Edwards's musings were interrupted by the ringing of his mobile telephone. It was "The Sheikh" calling from his office in the port city, on the eastern coastline, of this vast country. "Where are you staying?" he asked. He knew that Edwards was to fly to meet him the next day. Edwards told him the name of his hotel. "My brother would like to meet you," said "The Sheikh" and, since he had three brothers, added the name. Edwards stiffened; he knew that this brother held a very powerful position. He was the senior Government official in charge of purchasing all kinds of equipment and projects on behalf of and funded by the Government.

To meet this man would be the major achievement of Edwards's visit. "If you can be waiting in the hotel bar at six o'clock this evening," said the voice at the other end of the line. "He knows what you look like and he will find you." Edwards decided to return to his room for a one-hour siesta after his heavy lunch. When he got to his room, he checked his briefcase. It had not been disturbed.

# 5

At precisely ten minutes to six, Edwards took the lift down from his sixth-floor executive room to the hotel reception area on the ground floor and walked to the bar. He always liked to arrive a little early for a meeting, so as to be sure not to miss his guests and also to try to set the scene for the meeting, in his mind. He carefully selected a table for two in the middle of the room, which, he believed, made it more difficult for a listening device to have been installed. He sat down in the chair looking towards the entrance to the bar, so that he could perhaps identify his guest. An efficient waiter immediately appeared; Edwards ordered his favourite gin and tonic.

He sat and thought about the conversation to come; how could he approach the subject he wanted to speak about? He could start with the fact that he knew this man's brother quite well by now and the kind of things that he was talking to him about. Then he could turn the conversation to his own role. He was aware of one major potential trade deal with this country, which was of great interest to one of the companies he worked with. He could gently explore around that and the possibilities of closing this deal for Britain.

Edwards sat and slowly sipped his drink; he tried to make it last as long as possible. By now he had worked out what the approach might be; he knew that the company would be willing to offer certain other trade advantages to this country. These would include making part of their product here, which would mean investment, training and new employment prospects. By the time he looked at his watch again, he was surprised to see that it was already twenty minutes to seven. He got a little impatient; "why was it that other people were never on time, when he always tried to be?"

Without thinking, he had finished his drink; the waiter hovered into sight to take his empty glass away. "Another one, sir?" he asked. "Yes please," Edwards responded. He was getting a little annoyed at having to wait so long, and another gin and tonic, might just cheer him up.

His mind went back to his first trip to Africa; to the city of Enugu in Nigeria. The day after his rather frightening landing, he and his colleagues were due to have a meeting at ten o'clock in the morning with one of the relevant Ministers in the Regional Government of Anambra State, of which Enugu was a part. They had, of course, arrived at the Government building on time. It was a low, flat building, and the Minister's outer office had double doors which opened up onto a low veranda. The building was old and there was no air-conditioning. They were told, by his male Secretary, that the Minister was out, despite their having a firm meeting time fixed with him, and that he would arrive shortly.

There was one old armchair in the outer office for the use of visitors, and the oldest member of the party was selected to sit in it. Half-an-hour, one hour and then two hours went by, and still no Minister appeared. The room was getting hotter and hotter; outside, on the shaded veranda, there was, at least, a breath of air, but nowhere to sit. They persuaded the Minister's Secretary to open the double doors to the veranda so that they could get some cooler air into the stifling room. They could also now go outside, to try and recover a little from the heat, if they wished. The oldest member of the party offered his seat to one of his colleagues, who was beginning to feel tired, and after that, they decided to each have thirty minutes in the armchair, before giving it up to another colleague in turn.

So the wait went on; one of the group went out, at lunchtime, to try and find something to eat and drink. He came back with some sealed bottles of water to drink, but, he had failed to find anything to eat. They waited through the lunchtime and into the afternoon. The Minister's Secretary kept smiling at them, but was unable to say where his Minister was, or, when he would arrive. At last, at five o'clock, they decided to call it a day and agreed with the Minister's

Secretary, that they would return at ten o'clock the following morning.

This they did, only to find the Minister's office empty. "I suppose we could read all the secret Government papers on his desk," Edwards had joked with his colleagues. They opened the double doors to the veranda and took it in turn to sit in the easy chair and on the less comfortable chair of the Minister's Secretary, since he was not present to occupy it. They also took turns to get some cooler air out on the veranda. At around midday, the Minister suddenly arrived. He apologised that he had been travelling "up-State" and that he had not been informed about the meeting made with them for yesterday. "Where is my Secretary?" he asked his bemused visitors, but, they had to admit, that they had no idea where the man was!

Edwards looked at his watch again; it was now half-past seven. "This is Africa," thought Edwards to himself. "In Africa, time works in a different way and patience is everything!" Fortunately he had eaten a big lunch and could tough it out a little longer. He did not have the telephone number of "The Sheikh's" brother, but he did try calling "The Sheikh's" own mobile telephone. It went straight to Voicemail and he left a message. He finished his second drink and ordered another one. "When I finish this," he thought, "I will go to get dinner." By half-past eight, he had finished his third drink and decided that "The Sheikh's" brother was not going to put in an appearance that evening. Edwards retired to the dining room for a light dinner, and then took the lift upstairs to his room and went to bed.

# 6

Early the next morning, Edwards checked out of his hotel and took a taxi to the airport. He was booked on a domestic flight to the main port city of the country to meet "The Sheikh" himself. Despite what Hendriks had told him, he was not particularly worried at the moment about meeting "The Sheikh." After all, "The Sheikh's" other brother was Head of all of the various Intelligence Services in this country. Presumably, he would protect his brother and any of his visitors!

What Hendriks had said, however, was still worrying. "In the longer term," Hendriks had commented, "large changes could be coming here." He had also commented that "The Sheikh" was now clearly recognised as being too close to the country's Vice President, who himself was known for his corrupt ways. "This Government is known for its corruption, and the people are slowly beginning to realise, that they are not getting any improvements in their lives," Hendriks had told him. "The President is, perhaps, a reasonably honest man, but his Vice President is not, and the man that you are meeting, looks after most of the Vice President's business interests. He invests the money that the Vice President receives in bribes and can negotiate on his behalf for any new business dealings."

His aeroplane landed safely at the airport of the port city and Edwards was soon in a taxi to the hotel where "The Sheikh" had booked him a room. He had an appointment with "The Sheik" at three o'clock that afternoon at the man's plush offices in a blue, glass-fronted, office building which overlooked the large seaport. Edwards knew that "The Sheikh" was reasonably reliable. He would be there on time for the meeting, or he would turn up only a few minutes late. The more Edwards thought about the "no-show" of the previous evening's meeting, the more he realised that, "The Sheikh's" brother had probably decided that the hotel bar was too public a place to meet with Edwards.

As far as what Hendriks had told him was concerned, Edwards had now had the benefit of "sleeping on" the information that he had been given. Edwards found that often, in the morning, his brain had processed some new information that he had received, and that he could now make some kind of decision about it. He had decided that, such was the potential importance of his relationship with "The Sheikh," that he ought, with some caution, to continue their relationship and their discussions.

At five minutes to three, another taxi dropped Edwards off at the blue, glass-fronted office building. He took the lift up to the top floor, where "The Sheikh" had his office suite. His Receptionist showed him into the spacious office. "He won't be a minute," she said. Edwards had hardly had time to sit down, when the door opened. The dark, hypnotic eyes fixed on him, and the large mouth broke into a smile. "My dear chap," said "The Sheikh", "how nice to see you again." Edwards stood up and smiled back; somehow this man had acquired an English public school accent. They shook hands warmly.

But, Edwards knew, that this man had never attended such an exclusive English educational institution. He had once told Edwards the story of his education: after finishing at an ordinary school in this country, he had been selected for a scholarship to attend the prestigious Massachusetts Institute of Technology, where he had taken a degree in Electronics. He had then taken a Master's Degree in Business Administration, at the Sloan School of Management, which was also located in Boston. He had then finished off his further education, with two years at the K.G.B. College in Moscow! This was not unusual, as so-called "freedom fighters," were sometimes adopted and then supported through their education, by either the Russian or the American intelligence services, in the hope of cultivating future "agents of influence."

They sat down and two cups of strong coffee were brought in by the Receptionist. "The Sheikh" apologised, on behalf of his brother, for his non-appearance the previous evening, but he gave no reason for this. He then told Edwards about a potential deal he was working on; some second-hand warships had been recently bought for this country's Navy from a Western country. He was interested in equipping these with new electronic and weapons systems. He had already begun discussions with a French defence equipment and armaments manufacturer. Edwards realised, that he was being asked, indirectly, whether a British company might be interested in this potentially lucrative naval refitting contract?

They talked around the subject for half an hour, and, finally, "The Sheikh" indicated that he would be willing to work, as an alternative, with a British company, if Edwards could bring one forward. Edwards realised, very well, what would be involved in such an arrangement. But, as he represented the British Government, he wanted to carefully avoid any discussions of the need for, as one of his colleagues subtly put it, "paying for expensive piano lessons for their Minister's children."

Bribery and corruption were endemic in Africa and in many other parts of the world. Various nationalities had different ways of tackling this problem. The French, for example, treated the subject efficiently to start with but, often, then made the mistake, of trying to blackmail those that they had bribed, to work for French Intelligence. The Germans were more pragmatic and usually set up some anonymous, "numbered" bank accounts in the German-speaking part of Switzerland. The Russians usually arrived, in a particular country, with caseloads of money in United States dollar notes. The Americans, despite the fact that there was strict American legislation against such things, usually appointed a carefully selected local Agent to look after, at "arms-length", the illicit payments that, in many cases, were necessary to win American exports. The British took a cautious view, secretly establishing a small, carefully selected team of people, within their companies, to carry out this difficult and clandestine work.

They went on to discuss some other topics, including one in which Edwards had an interest. That was attracting a favourable reaction to export proposals, by companies adding investment, training and other incentives to their bids. This could promote genuine economic development within this country, in return for British trade deals. "The Sheikh" was really helpful in his remarks about this matter and, as always, Edwards was amazed by the man's intelligence and scope of knowledge.

At about five-thirty, "The Sheikh" indicated that their meeting was at an end. He stood up and then invited Edwards to dinner. "My Receptionist will now call you a taxi to get you back to your hotel," he said charmingly. "I have another meeting now for about an hour. At seven o'clock, I will collect you from your hotel and take you out to dinner."

# 7

That evening, "The Sheikh" entertained Edwards to dinner at a first-class Indian restaurant in the port city. When they arrived together in "The Sheikh's" luxury, air-conditioned car, they were immediately shown to their table, where two more of his guests were already waiting for his arrival. "The Sheikh" introduced them to Edwards; they appeared to be two fairly prominent businessmen from this city. They all partook of an excellent spicy meal, washed down with the local beer. After the food and over coffee and liqueurs, "The Sheikh" offered all of his guests a large Havana cigar. He appeared to like these larger cigars; Edwards could not help but wonder if they were a replacement, in some way, for the fact that he could no longer father children?

Throughout the evening, various other suited men had wandered in and out of the restaurant; each one appeared to know "The Sheikh" and, in one way or another, acknowledged him. Some even came over to their table to be introduced to his guests and have a brief discussion. Edwards could not help feeling that, somehow, he was present in the Imperial Court of some powerful Oriental Potentate!

The next morning, Edwards began his journey back to London; first the short flight back to the country's main city, and then the wait for the non-stop, overnight flight back to Heathrow. "The Sheikh" had said to him, that he would be in London again the following month, and asked him if he could arrange some meetings with people who were possible business partners for him. As soon as he arrived home, Edwards began to plan for the man's visit.

Edwards first went to see Tim, who was the Managing Director of a company which specialised in discreet investigations, the protection of branded products against counterfeiting and the training of Customs and Police Forces in developing countries. Tim, who had left British Customs and Excise in a senior position, had formed his company some years before, with a retired Metropolitan Police officer as his business partner. It was now quite a successful company and, given the level of inefficiency, pilfering and corruption within the major port in "The Sheikh's" city, Edwards felt that there might be an opportunity for Tim's company to get involved.

When "The Sheikh" arrived the following month, the meeting that Edwards had planned was duly held, and Edwards and Tim met with "The Sheikh" at his luxury London hotel. The discussion went well, and Tim made some very valid points, about how his company could help with some of the difficulties experienced by the major port in "The Sheikh's" home city. Coming out of the hotel, after the meeting, Tim and Edwards decided to walk the short distance back to Tim's office, so that they could review the meeting together and plan their next move. Edwards was surprised when Tim glanced behind him several times.

"We are being followed!" hissed Tim.

"Who by?" asked Edwards. "Is it their lot or ours?"

"I can't tell," Tim replied.

"Don't worry," said Edwards. "They can follow us back to your office, and much good will it do them!"

Edwards had to believe that Tim was right; after all, he knew that Tim had been trained in counter-surveillance techniques, during his time at Customs and Excise. But Edwards had experienced close surveillance before, during some of his business trips abroad, to countries that were then behind the "Iron Curtain", and when he had worked in Turkey. He had become a little blasé about these experiences; after all he was just doing his job in trying to help British companies export their goods and services overseas. What was wrong with that and, provided that you did not compromise yourself, what could anyone prove against you?

The following morning, Edwards had arranged for "The Sheikh" to meet the Chairman and Board of Directors of a major London company. They met in the company's Board Room and, after introducing him, Edwards had allowed "The Sheikh" to "take the floor." The man had stood up and walked to a white-board at the head of the long Board Room table. Taking a felt-tipped pen, he had made his presentation. Speaking without notes, but using the white-board to perfectly illustrate his points, he had entranced his audience for over an hour with a vivid description of his country and how they could work with him, to develop business there. Edwards had watched the faces of the Chairman and the Board members carefully; they had appeared totally won over by this man, and were anxious to follow up on this meeting, as soon as possible, and do some business with him.

After this meeting, Edwards took "The Sheikh" out for lunch. Edwards was by now a member of a London club that was close to the centre of British Government power in Whitehall. It was a large and impressive building and had a cosy bar and a fine dining room. Over the meal, he felt that he had to compliment this man on his presentation that morning.

"We must get some business going between us," was the reply. "The Vice President will be here in three weeks for two days on a private visit, and I would like you to entertain him and introduce him to some interesting people."

Edwards nodded, but then he began to wonder what he could do with the Vice President of a major African country, for two whole days? By now, he felt that he was experienced in the "craft" of Government Relations and in International Business and Trade, but, just by himself, he had never looked after the Vice President of another country before. He was due to arrive on a private visit to London in just three weeks' time! That was not much time at all, to arrange a program of interesting, relevant meetings for this senior visitor.

# 8

It was, therefore, with some trepidation, that Edwards went on the appointed morning and at the time agreed, to collect the Vice President at his luxury, London hotel. He had been told that he was registered under another name, for security reasons, and that he did not have with him the usual collection of security men, as this was a private visit to London. Using the name that he had been given, he asked for the guest at the hotel reception and then sat down, on a sofa, facing the lifts, and waited.

After a few minutes, the door of one of the lifts opened and there was the smiling, black face that Edwards immediately recognised from the photographs of this man that he had seen. Edwards had wondered how he should address him; should he address him as "Mr. Vice President"? Instead, he approached him and said, "Good Morning, sir. My name is Edwards and I think that you are expecting me." The Vice President was charm itself; his smile became even broader and he shook Edwards's proffered hand firmly, using both of his hands. He was immaculately dressed in an expensive-looking, well-tailored, three-piece suit. He wore a smart shirt and a sober tie; his black shoes were well burnished.

In front of him, Edwards felt a little inferior; he had on his usual off-the-peg two-piece suit and, he remembered, he had forgotten to brush his shoes that morning! They sat down together on the sofa. Edwards made the usual polite enquiries about the comfort of his hotel and expressed the hope that he had enjoyed a good flight to

London, the previous day. He explained the program that he had arranged for the Vice President for the next two days. The man stopped him. "I am very sorry, Mr. Edwards," he said politely, "but, tomorrow morning, I have a meeting at my bank and then another meeting and then a lunch. I can see you with your friend tomorrow afternoon and then for dinner."

The Vice President seemed to be setting his own itinerary for his visit. Then he added, "This evening, too, I am unfortunately busy." Was there perhaps a gleam in his eye as he said this? He then winked at Edwards! Edwards could not help remembering that this man was allowed, in accordance with his tribal tradition, numerous wives. At the last count, he had read, the Vice President had had six wives. He was also rumoured to have had many lady friends and to have fathered over twenty children!

Edwards escorted the Vice President to a taxi waiting in the rank outside the hotel. Then, as they drove, he apologised, as he had to use his mobile telephone to cancel several of the planned meetings and to rearrange one of them. They pulled up at the entrance to the impressive building where the company "The Sheikh" had visited, only three weeks before, had their headquarters. On entering, they were immediately escorted into a private lift and taken up to the top floor dining room. There the Chairman and three of his Directors were waiting; all of them greeted the Vice President and Edwards with great respect.

Over aperitifs, the Vice President was shown the magnificent views of London from the large picture windows. They sat down at the table, which was covered in a pristine tablecloth, gleaming silver cutlery and sparkling cut-glass. A light soup was served, followed by an appetising fish course and then traditional roast beef, accompanied by vegetables and, of course, Yorkshire pudding. With each dish was served its own, specially selected, wine, and, with the dessert, was served a sweet Hungarian Tokaji. Edwards observed that the Vice President particularly seemed to like the excellent Claret that had been served with the roast beef and he had indicated, to one of the waiters, that he would like to continue drinking it. A newly opened bottle of Claret was brought and put beside him, so that he could help himself.

As was polite, it was only when coffee, liqueurs and cigars were served, that the company representatives got down to business. The Chairman began.

"We were very impressed with Mr. ------ when he paid us a visit a few weeks ago," he said, naming "The Sheikh."

The Vice President smiled. "Yes, he is a very clever man," he said. "I would be very happy to support any project that your company had in mind, if he recommended it to me."

To Edwards, the Vice President's meaning was clear; some kind of a deal to benefit him had to be arranged with "The Sheikh" and then all things became possible! A discussion then ensued about a number of potential projects, each Director making his contribution. The Vice President nodded at each one; Edwards noticed that he was careful not to approve of any particular project. At the end of the list, the Vice President smiled again. "The more the merrier!" he said, laughing.

Outside, after the lunch was over, they took another taxi to Edwards's Club; there Edwards had quickly arranged for Tim to visit. The Vice President enjoyed a teapot of Earl Grey, while Tim and Edwards indulged in several cups of mellow Columbian coffee. Again, the Vice

President listened politely, while Tim outlined his plan for his company to assist in the re-organisation and training of, the personnel in the country's major port. At the end, the Vice President looked at Edwards; "Again, you must discuss this with our mutual colleague," he said. Edwards, of course, understood him to mean that he must now speak to "The Sheikh" about this possible project.

The next afternoon, Edwards was waiting in the reception area of another five-star hotel, where the Vice President had told him that he was having lunch that day. Soon he appeared; he seemed ebullient and to have had another "good lunch." Edwards resisted the idea of asking the man how he had enjoyed his previous evening! Outside, they climbed into a taxi; "Middle Temple," Edwards told the driver. Edwards was taking the Vice President to meet one of Edwards's oldest friends. Brian was a senior international barrister whose education Edwards always joked about. "He had an awful education," Edwards used to say. "He went to Eton, Oxford and then Harvard!"

It was true; who Brian didn't know was not worth knowing. He was called in to advise on many unusual or high-profile situations and was paid extremely well for doing so. One day, over a "liquid lunch," Brian had told Edwards, in confidence, of a recent incident where a Government Minister had been found naked by the Police on Hampstead Heath, in the arms of another man. Both men had been taken to a Central London Police Station and, after a quick consultation with Scotland Yard's Special Branch, which handled such sensitive matters, Brian had been called at home and asked to attend as a legal adviser. Needless to say, he had managed to resolve the incident, without any charges being brought, and without any embarrassment falling on the Government.

Brian had also served as a Legal Adviser to several overseas governments and a number of Heads of State, so Edwards thought it opportune to introduce him to the Vice President. At the barrier that blocked off the entrance to Middle Temple Lane, Edwards stopped the taxi. "If it is alright with you, sir, it is a nice day and we can walk there from here," he said. In fact, he wanted to show the Vice President some of the sights of the Middle Temple as they walked.

The Honourable Society of the Middle Temple is one of the four Inns of Court in London that are entitled to call their members to the "English Bar" as barristers. They can then appear, at a senior level, to represent clients, in the English courts of law. In the thirteenth century, the Inns of Court originated as hostels and schools for student lawyers. The Middle Temple now occupies the western part of the grounds of "The Temple", which was originally the London headquarters of the Knights Templar, until they were dissolved in 1312.

# 9

The Vice President and Edwards walked up the slight hill of the cobbled Middle Temple Lane from the River Thames Embankment. As they passed, Edwards pointed out the sights. To their left was Middle Temple Hall; begun in 1562, it was the finest example of an Elizabethan building in London. He mentioned how he had been entertained by Brian to lunch there several times. A diversion to the right brought them to the Temple Church, built by the Knights Templar in the twelfth century. Based on a circular design, it was supposed to represent a copy of the first Temple in Jerusalem, built by King Solomon. It contained the tombs of many of the Knights Templar. Finally, Edwards took the Vice President to the Fountain

Court, to see the oldest water fountain still working in London. This fountain was mentioned by Charles Dickens in his novel Martin Chuzzlewit and, around its more modern base, were inscribed the words written by Dickens to describe it.

They climbed the old, creaking wooden staircase to Brian's Chambers, the place where he worked when not representing some client in court. They were received by the Clerk, the chief of administration for these Chambers, which included offices for several other barristers that Brian worked with as business partners. They were shown into Brian's office with its view, through the old sash windows, of the trees in one of the garden squares of the Middle Temple. To the right of Brian's large desk, which was piled high with papers, was a fireplace with a seventeenth-century wooden surround ornately carved by the celebrated Dutch-British master, Grinling Gibbons. One day, Brian had mentioned to Edwards, that this surround had been valued at one million pounds, but he still kept his spare ashtrays on it, and it was usually covered with a layer of dust and cigarette ash.

In this room, Edwards always felt that he was back in the time of Dickens; he sat back and listened to the conversation between Brian and the Vice President. Both men were trying to outdo each other in their charm offensive; names of prominent African politicians whom he knew, tumbled out of Brian's mouth. Then several other Heads of State were mentioned. The Vice President looked suitably impressed as Brian outlined the legal services he could provide at a high level to the Government that the Vice President represented. After one hour, the meeting was over.

"You will excuse me, but I have an urgent brief I must put together by this evening," said Brian.

"Not at all," said the Vice President. "It has been a great pleasure to meet you, and I am sure that we may indeed call upon you for your services."

They all shook hands and then Edwards led the Vice President down the ancient stairs and out of the Middle Temple, through the almost-hidden entrance onto The Strand. Edwards hailed a taxi to take the Vice President back to his hotel. He was to meet him there later, to take him out to dinner with another British company, with whom he had carefully planned another trade opportunity.

The dinner that evening was an intimate affair; just the Vice President, Edwards, and a senior director of a company that owned several leading hotels and casinos. Their business was highly profitable and they owned probably the leading London casino, where the meeting took place. Edwards remembered well the opening scenes of one of the James Bond films, which were set in this very casino. It had a superb restaurant and bar; the older part of the building was the original house built by a leading, Jewish banking family. The opulent gaming rooms were set on the first floor, up an antique, sweeping staircase.

The Director of the company, who was called Roger, was well known to Edwards. He was a retired senior Scotland Yard detective, who had now taken on the role of keeping this hotel and casino group on the "straight and narrow". He ran the entire "security operation" for the whole chain; everybody from doormen to the pretty, but very carefully selected, female croupiers they employed, came under his responsibility. To protect the group's casino business, total surveillance, within each of their casinos, was important.

One day, Roger had taken Edwards into the "control room" of one of their London casinos. There, in front of a bank of television screens, linked to numerous CCTV cameras, sat a highly trained team. They watched for any cheating and were ready to immediately intervene, if they spotted anything like that happening, or any unusual patterns of behaviour or gambling activity taking place. Through hidden microphones, they could also eavesdrop on any conversations taking place in the casino.

During his police career, Roger had been called in many times by foreign police forces and had advised them on difficult security, counter-terrorism and kidnap and hostage situations. This was the role he had also carried out in London and elsewhere in Britain. Because of his wide experience, he was also involved in the international marketing aspects of his present employer, particularly when they wished to open a new hotel or casino overseas. Edwards knew that they were interested in opening a new hotel and casino in the major port city in the Vice President's country, which Edwards had now visited several times. This was the reason that Edwards had arranged this evening meeting.

Charmingly, over drinks followed by an excellent dinner, Roger gave a short presentation on their business and then turned to the proposed project he had in mind. The Vice President, as always, listened politely and carefully. When Roger had finished, he asked some very pertinent questions, that showed that he had understood the position completely. Then, the Vice President turned to Edwards, "Another one for our mutual colleague!" he said.

After coffee, liqueurs and cigars had been served. Roger then suggested that maybe the Vice President would like to visit the gaming rooms upstairs; the man beamed and said that he would very much like to do so. Edwards knew that Roger would fund the first bet for the Vice President, if this man wanted to play Roulette, Poker,

Blackjack or Baccarat, which were all on offer. They climbed the wide staircase, with the beautifully carved handrail, and entered the double doors to the main gaming room. The cut-glass chandeliers were hung low, to give sufficient light to the green-baized tables, where the card games could be played. As always, the main crowd of gamblers were seated around the Roulette table. Roger opened several doors and showed them inside the ornate private salons, where very rich clients could gamble with their close friends, away from the less wealthy crowd in the main gaming room.

The Vice President took it all in, but he did not seem to want to gamble. What clearly interested him more, were the beautiful, smartly dressed female croupiers, who stood or sat at every gaming table!

# 10

That night, Edwards thankfully delivered the Vice President back to his hotel. It was already well after midnight. The man was due to fly back to his own country, the following morning. As always, as they said goodbye, the man was charming. "Thank you, Mr. Edwards, for an interesting visit," he said, shaking Edwards's hand in both of his. "You really must go and see our mutual colleague again and discuss all this with him."

Edwards took the same taxi home; thankfully, the fare would be paid by his employer. In the taxi, he mused to himself. "A successful visit?" he wondered. "But now, a lot for me to follow up on." He would have to think carefully, and discuss again each potential project, with the people whom he had identified to promote their business and trade with the Vice President's country. Only then could he think about returning to see "The Sheik" again. But did he really want to do that?

The Vice President had proved to be a very rapacious man. Edwards did not like this business of bribery and corruption, but it was widespread throughout the world. If British companies did not do it, they would just lose out to firms from other counties, who were only too happy to bribe their way to business. Britain could take a "moral stand", like the Americans had done; but so often what happened then was that corruption went even more "underground" and companies found even more devious ways to do it, in order to get business. It was not that Britain could honestly take such a "moral stand"; Britain was also corrupt! It was just that it was hidden so well and people never talked about it. Edwards knew of cases where senior members, of several companies, had "stolen" from their companies or from their company's customers. Usually, it was just "hushed up", and nothing happened to these "white-collar criminals!"

When he arrived home, it was after two o'clock in the morning; he let himself into the house quietly. Fortunately, his wife and two children were all soundly asleep. He would have less than four hours sleep, before his clock radio would wake him up with the six o'clock BBC World Service News. He listened to this news every morning, so that he always knew about major world events. "Such are the joys of promoting international trade and investment!" he thought, as his head hit the pillow. He was almost immediately asleep.

Over the next two weeks, Edwards had follow-up meetings with the four parties whom he had introduced to the Vice President. He tried to learn their true reaction to this visit and their current thoughts on going forward with the matters that had been discussed. The most enjoyable one of these meetings was, as always, with Brian. They met in an old, Mayfair wine bar in Shepherd Market, one of Brian's favourite haunts. Over several bottles of very good French red wine, they discussed the Vice President and his close business relationship with "The Sheikh."

Brian was "worldly-wise." "It worries me," he said. "The politics and the goings-on in that country make what is currently going on in Russia look like a Vicarage tea party!" Edwards well remembered what Hendriks had told him, and could only but agree with Brian's concise comment. The whole situation that he found himself in, had begun to worry Edwards and the promotion of British trade, into such a corrupt and, indeed, possibly unstable political situation, was beginning to seem somewhat unwise.

It was only a week later that he began to read in the newspapers of certain rumours. They were contained in articles about "The Sheikh's" country. Edwards had to flick through several newspapers every morning, just to be aware of what was happening in world affairs. Just two days later, the BBC World Service News woke him up, and brought him the startling announcement that the President of "The Sheikh's" country had just decided to dismiss his Vice President on the grounds of corruption! Much more was to follow. Within a month, "The Sheikh" himself had been arrested and charged with several counts of bribery and corruption. He was imprisoned awaiting trial, which, in his country, with its inefficient legal system, could take some time to come to court.

Edwards was very embarrassed; he discussed the situation with Brian and Tim, whom he classed as friends, but was unwilling to make contact again with Roger or the major company that he had visited, with the former Vice President, so very recently. He did not know what kind of reaction he would get now from these two established British companies. In view of this news, they must think of him as a fool!

Months went by, before reports of "The Sheikh's" trial began to emerge. Edwards tried to follow the story carefully. It became clear that "The Sheik's" education was a lie; he had not attended the prestigious institutions in Boston that he had mentioned to Edwards, nor the K.G.B. College in Moscow! Instead, he had been caught cheating on a final examination paper, in what was a Technical College in his own country. He had then been asked to leave the college, without any qualification being awarded to him.

In court, he admitted some of the bribery allegations he was charged with, although he tried to portray the former Vice President as innocent. "He had been doing all this just to benefit himself," he was reported to have said. The former Vice President tried to distance himself from this man and from the allegations that were flying around. Indeed, he did not appear in court in "The Sheikh's" defence, although he admitted that he knew him. But, he said, he had never authorised him to act on his behalf. It became clear to Edwards, that the former Vice President was "hanging "The Sheikh" out to dry!"

The conclusion of the trial was almost inevitable; "The Sheikh" was found guilty on all counts and sentenced to 15 years in jail. Edwards felt rather sorry for him; jails in his country were not very comfortable places, and many prisoners, on long sentences, after a few years, just died there. Time went by and Edwards almost forgot what he had been involved in until, one day, he met the old friend, who had introduced him to Hendriks. Their talk turned to the former Vice President.

"Did you know that he is back in favour again?" asked his friend. "He used the man you call "The Sheikh" as his "fall guy." He is now tipped to be elected, next month, as head of the ruling party. When the current President retires, which is expected soon, he will become President. He will just buy or threaten his way to the top!"

Just as his friend had predicted, within the space of six months, the disgraced former Vice President, became President of his country. One day, a few months later, Edwards was speaking to his friend again on the telephone. "You may be interested to know," he said to Edwards, "that the man you called "The Sheikh," has just been released after two-and-a-half years in jail. On the grounds of his ill health. However, his health seems fine. He has already been seen playing golf on his favourite course and spending freely in the bars and restaurants of his home city."

"He says, that he is considering taking some kind of legal action against the new President, for leaving him "to take the rap,"" Edwards's friend went on. "But I don't think that will happen, do you? If he tries to do that, he will have some nasty road accident, or he will be conveniently shot dead by someone trying to rob him. Or he may just disappear, forever! Whatever happens to him, the police will be ordered not to investigate." Edwards found, that from his own experience of that country, he could do nothing else but to agree with his old friend.

THE END

# Tremors

-

*"If there is one eternal truth of politics, it is that there are always a dozen good reasons for doing nothing."*

— **John le Carre**

# 1

"I have recently met the most dangerous man in the world!"

Edwards sat bolt upright in his chair and looked at the man who had just said these words. The man was dressed in a business suit, white shirt and tie; he had a sallow complexion with jet black hair and his body was thin and distinguished by quick, rather nervous, movements. He was being very serious about what he had said.

They were seated opposite each other, at a small round table, in the bar of a private Club near to Saint James's Park in London. The Club was now housed in what had once been a fine private residence, and it had, since it's founding in 1870, always been closely affiliated to the Conservative Party. On one wall of the room, a photograph of the Second World War Prime Minister, Sir Winston Churchill, glowered down. On the opposite wall was a fetching portrait of the former Conservative Prime Minister, Margaret Thatcher.

The lunchtime rush was now over, and the Club was quiet. Earlier, Edwards had met there with his friend Derek, who was a member of this Club. They had had a plain and reasonably inexpensive lunch together, complemented by a bottle of good, red wine, in the small dining room of the Club. Over the meal, Derek, who had known Edwards now for many years, had told him about this man. Edwards knew that Derek had many contacts, in various parts of the world, so he did not ask his friend how he had met him. Derek had arranged for the man to come to the Club, after their lunch, and, having briefly introduced them, he had left.

"The fewer people who hear what he has to say, the better," Derek had said quietly, into Edwards's ear, before leaving.

It was the late 1990s; Edwards was now working for an organisation, promoted by the British Government, to help British companies export overseas. He was working as a temporary civil servant, but on a grade senior enough, to be paid an adequate salary. By now he had a long experience of the world of international business and finance; first, a decade in banking in the City of London, and then he had been employed for over ten years by a major construction group to advise on all matters financial. For that group, he had travelled to many parts of the world, and he felt that he was now well qualified to advise other British companies on finding overseas markets and how to finance exports.

It was during one of these overseas visits, that he had made for his construction group, that he had first met Derek. That visit had been to the city of Enugu in Eastern Nigeria in 1983. Derek had been there, too, representing a London firm of surveyors, who were working, together with Edwards's employers, on a major construction project in that city. They had become friends and, over the years, had travelled together to various places, including an extensive visit to South East Asia. This had taken them to Thailand, Singapore, Indonesia and Hong Kong. Their birthdays were only a week apart, and they had celebrated Edwards's birthday, over an expensive bottle of Champagne, in the bar of the Hilton Hotel in Jakarta, accompanied by the music of a traditional, Javanese Gamelan band, who were playing in there that evening. Derek's birthday had been celebrated in his hotel room, in Hong Kong, over a bottle of good whisky.

Edwards's current organisation consisted of a mix of businessmen and civil servants, the latter seconded from their respective Government Departments. Among them was one man, whom Edwards had got to know well. His name was Michael, and he was a senior serving Intelligence Officer. He had access, if required, to his senior colleagues in the various British intelligence agencies. The purpose of his position was to try and give British companies the "competitive edge" in exporting, particularly to difficult countries. High-level executives of companies could ask this man specific questions, or for more general advice about certain situations. They could also have the benefit of confidential briefings, if this was thought necessary.

This was nothing more than Britain's competitors did: the French were well-known for the close links between major French companies and their intelligence services. The Americans, who spent enormous amounts of money on their intelligence services, always arranged for the confidential briefing of senior executives, who belonged to some of their major commercial companies. This was done either in the United States, before overseas visits were made, or within the American Embassy in the relevant capital city of the country concerned.

Edwards and Derek by now knew each other very well and trusted each other. One day, Edwards had quietly mentioned to Derek about Michael's role within his organisation and had outlined what might be on offer. Derek had expressed an interest in meeting Michael, and Edwards had arranged a social get-together one evening, between the three of them, in a wine bar close to his offices near Whitehall. When he had telephoned Edwards, a few days ago, Derek had been somewhat mysterious about the purpose of their meeting today. But, over lunch, he had mentioned the name of Edwards's colleague and this had then led to a description of the man that Derek was about to introduce to Edwards.

"He studied journalism," Derek had told Edwards. "But he also speaks fluent Arabic. After his studies, he worked for various newspapers in Arab countries. He then moved back to London and now works for an Arab-language newspaper here. His newspaper has been very critical of various Arab regimes, including that of Saddam Hussein. As a result, he is now very much in fear of his life. He claims that his wife was killed in London, some years ago, by the use of a rare poison administered by the Iraqi foreign intelligence service. They, of course, deny it completely, and the case has never received any publicity. The police and the authorities here claim that she died of natural causes, and they have refused to investigate any further."

# 2

By now, Edwards knew quite a lot about the world of intelligence and security; he knew that the last thing that the British authorities would admit to was that a foreign intelligence service had successfully murdered someone on British soil. The assassination of the Bulgarian dissident writer, Georgi Markov, in 1978, had become public knowledge, only because of the statements that the dying man had made to his BBC colleagues, and to the doctors in the London hospital where he was admitted. He had taken four days to die, from an injection into the back of his leg, of the deadly poison ricin. This had been administered by a Bulgarian Government agent, who had jabbed Markov with the sharpened end of an umbrella, containing a tiny phial of the poison, as he was walking over Waterloo Bridge.

Even successful operations, by foreign criminal gangs, seemed to have been kept hidden where possible. It took the City of London Police, over twenty years, to admit that the death by hanging of the Italian banker Roberto Calvi, under Blackfriars Bridge in 1982, had been a murder carried out by the Italian Mafia. This was despite the fact that various forensic studies, carried out overseas, had clearly identified that this was a case of murder and that the Italian authorities had concluded, some years before, that the death of this man in London, had been a Mafia "contract killing."

Edwards also knew about the capability of the authorities in various overseas countries to hide the truth. Some two years before, he had taken part in a conference to try and promote exports from selected companies in Northern Ireland. That unfortunate part of the United Kingdom had, by then, experienced years of terrorist attacks by the Irish Republican Army. Over lunch, Edwards had met the Director of a construction company who now specialised in building bomb-proof buildings and protecting existing buildings from bomb attacks. In confidence, this man informed Edwards that he had recently returned from New York where, for months, he had been asked to advise the Federal Bureau of Investigation after the bombing of the North Tower of the World Trade Centre in February 1993.

This attack had involved the detonation of a van filled with explosives in the basement car park of that building and had resulted in the deaths of six people and the injury of over a thousand. Only very slowly, did the details of this plot and its expected terrible aftermath, become public knowledge. What this man had quietly told Edwards had been horrifying and had never received any full publicity.

Having worked in the construction industry, Edwards knew that the design and building of the "Twin Towers" of the World Trade Centre had, at the time, been unique. In order to save on both time and costs, the "Twin Towers" had been built, using an innovative framed tube structure, with numerous closely spaced perimeter columns, to take the weight of the building. While there were also core columns in the centre of the building, to help take up the "gravity load," as it was called, the normal steel-based skyscraper skeleton structure had not been used. This design resulted in these very tall buildings having certain additional structural risks, and, it was these risks, that the terrorists, later identified as being linked to Al-Qaeda, had exploited.

The Ulsterman had told Edwards that, in the New York apartment used by the terrorist gang, copies of the very detailed engineering plans of the World Trade Centre had been discovered. Furthermore, a copy of a professional engineering study had also been found. This study the terrorists had paid for, using a respectable "front company." It had been carried out by a leading firm of structural engineers. The study identified the exact point, in the basement of the North Tower, where a bomb, of a particular strength, could be placed, to demolish the building. The terrorist plan was to demolish the North Tower, in such a way, that, it would hit the South Tower as it collapsed and bring that building down as well.

The timing of the explosion was planned to take place in the middle of the morning, so that both buildings would be fully occupied. That way, the terrorists would achieve the maximum number of fatalities. "Their estimates showed that, if they were successful, they would cause up to eight hundred thousand casualties," the man had whispered to Edwards.

Fortunately, the terrorists had made a fundamental mistake; they had packed their explosives into a van, rather than a car. When they tried to get this vehicle into the right position, in the underground car park of the North Building, the low roof of the car park had prevented them from placing their van at the exact point, designated in the engineering report, which they had paid for. When it was detonated, the bomb had shaken the building and caused some casualties, but it had failed to bring the building crashing down, as had been planned.

It was only when the full details of the attack had to be made available in court, that the terrorists' careful preparations, and the expert advice that they had received, become clear. Even then, the full horrible intent of their plans, was never fully made public. In 1994, four men were convicted of carrying out the bombing, and in 1997, two more men, including the leader of the group, Ramzi Yousef, were convicted and sent to prison.

Ramzi Yousef had been born in Kuwait, had studied electrical engineering in Swansea, South Wales, and had then received training in bomb-making, while at an Al-Qaeda camp in Afghanistan. He had fled from the United States to Pakistan, after the World Trade Centre bombing, and, from there, was involved in several plots to try to bring down civilian airliners. He was finally arrested in Pakistan in 1995 and extradited to the United States, where he stood trial on multiple charges. In 1997, he was finally sentenced to be jailed for life, without parole, plus another 240 years in jail.

# 3

"Call me Richard," the man had said to Edwards, just after they had sat down in the bar of the Club. He had refused any alcoholic drink, but had taken a coffee. Edwards had joined him in his choice, as he had wanted a clear head, after the wine at lunch, to hear exactly what this man had to tell him. It seemed that Richard first wanted to get Edwards's sympathy; he began by telling Edwards the story of the death of his wife a few years before. She had left their London flat one morning, as she always did, to buy fresh bread at the local bakery, which she always used. On returning home, she had eaten some of this bread. A few minutes later, she complained of feeling unwell; by the early afternoon, she had taken to her bed, with a high temperature, a headache and swelling joints.

By late afternoon, Richard had become worried and called a doctor, who had arrived in the evening. He had diagnosed a viral infection and prescribed some painkillers, but that was all. But her condition had worsened, and, overnight, she had become unconscious. In the early hours of the morning, Richard had called an ambulance. She was taken to hospital, but they had been unable to save her. Before dawn, the following morning, she was dead.

Edwards thought that he had to express his sympathy which, by now, he genuinely felt for this man. "How awful for this to happen so quickly," he had said.

"But I suspected it was not a natural death straight away," said Richard. "I had been afraid for our lives for some time. I had been warned that, unless I stopped criticising the Saddam Hussein regime, we would be harmed. But stupidly, I had thought that we would be safe in England. She liked fresh bread, and, when she got home that morning, she ate some and then began feeling ill. Somehow, the Iraqis must have poisoned it!"

"But did they carry out a post-mortem?" asked Edwards.

"Yes," said Richard, "but the result was that she had died of natural causes, from a viral infection. I tried to get them to test the remaining bread, but they refused to do so. I had no money to get the bread tested independently. Nobody would listen to me, when I said that she had been murdered by the Iraqi Intelligence Service!"

Edwards began to feel that this man was genuine; he had been in fear of his life and clearly believed that his wife had been poisoned. By now, his experience had taught him, to sit back and listen to what people wanted to tell him. But he was not prepared for what Richard revealed next about himself.

"I returned, a few weeks ago, from Afghanistan," Richard told him. "There I had, with great difficulty, arranged to carry out an important interview. First, I had to be led through the mountains, dressed in Afghan clothes. It was one of the most frightening trips that I have ever made in my life. I did not know, whether I could really trust, the men that I was with. When we arrived at our destination, I had to stay for four days, until he was ready to meet me. It was very primitive there and freezing cold at night."

"But where were you?" queried Edwards.

"In the Tora Bora Mountains," replied Richard.

"But who did you go so far to interview?" asked Edwards.

"He met me at last in his cave," replied Richard. "His name is Osama bin Laden. I have recently met the most dangerous man in the world!"

Edwards had heard of the name of the head of the terrorist group Al-Qaeda; he was now paying the closest attention to everything that Richard had to say. "What was he like?" he asked.

"He was very friendly towards me," Richard replied. "He had heard that I was an opponent of Saddam Hussein and he hates him, almost as much as he now hates the Saudi Royal Family. That was the only reason that he decided to give me an interview."

Edwards knew that Osama bin Laden was now the "black sheep" of the Bin Laden family, which had moved from Yemen to, what would become Saudi Arabia, before the First World War. Osama's father was Mohammed bin Awad bin Laden, who, despite being poor and uneducated, had founded his own construction business in 1930. He had come to the attention of the first King of Saudi Arabia, Abdul Aziz Ibn Saud, who had asked him to carry out numerous construction projects for the Saudi Royal Family. He became so close to the Royal Family that, in 1964, the then King Faisal, had issued a royal decree, awarding all future Saudi-government construction projects to bin Laden's construction company. Using this exclusive position, the bin Laden's had become the richest family in Saudi Arabia, outside of the Royal Family itself.

When his father had died in an aircraft accident in 1967, Osama had no fewer than 55 brothers and sisters from his father's 22 different wives. Each child, including Osama, was rumoured to have been left twenty-five to thirty million United States dollars from the over five-billion-dollar personal fortune that, by then, their father had accumulated. After leaving a Saudi university in 1979, Osama moved to Pakistan and then joined the Mujahideen. These guerrilla fighters were then strongly supported by Western countries, as they were fighting against the invasion of Afghanistan by the Soviet Union.

Using his inheritance, he helped fund the Mujahideen and also gained further financial support for them from the Arab world, using his many contacts. In May 1988, the Soviet Union began to pull out its troops from Afghanistan, and it was in that year, too, that Osama founded Al-Qaeda, which he claimed was set up to defend Islam from attacks by the Western world.

The Iraqi invasion of Kuwait in 1990, gave Saddam Hussein's forces the opportunity to push towards the oil-rich Eastern Province of Saudi Arabia. The threat to that country was considered real, and Osama bin Laden offered his Mujahideen fighters, to help defend Saudi Arabia. But his offer was spurned by the Saudi Royal Family, and Osama then criticised them for allowing Western armed forces into Saudi Arabia to defend it. As a result, in 1992, he was banned from returning to Saudi Arabia, the country of his birth.

Richard was continuing his story: "He is now determined to attack Western forces in the Middle East and the Western World generally," he was saying. "He also wants to undermine the Saudi Royal Family, whenever he can." Edwards was, by now, listening very carefully to what this man was telling him.

"You know that he lived for about four years in the Sudan, but he has now moved his base, back to Afghanistan," continued Richard. "He hates the Americans, and all the other Western countries, who have troops in the Middle East. He is certainly now the most dangerous man in the world, as far as the Western countries are concerned. He is using his money and his contacts, to promote attacks on the Western world, as much as he can."

Edwards had sensed that all of this, was leading somewhere, but he had wisely kept silent and let this man tell his story "in his own time." Edwards had been thinking; "This man will surely ask me for something. He is leading up to it." Richard was now, finally, coming to the point of their meeting.

"Your friend told me that he trusts you completely, and that you have contacts with British Intelligence," Richard said. "I know that Osama bin Laden is now travelling regularly, by a private jet, between the Sudan, where he is winding up his business affairs, and Afghanistan.

I have, through my contacts, prior access to the flight plans of that aircraft. I would be willing to supply these flight plans to British Intelligence, so that they can intercept this aircraft. They can either shoot it down or, if they wish, force it to land at a suitable airport, so that they can then arrest bin Laden. Then they can interrogate him. Could you please arrange an introduction for me to British intelligence so that, together, we can put an end to this very dangerous man?"

# 4

Edwards felt a very heavy burden of responsibility, as he left the Club, having said goodbye to Richard and promising that he would do all that he could to help him. It was just a short London Underground train journey back to his office, close to the centre of government power in Whitehall. When he arrived there, he sat behind his desk, and thought about the meeting he had just had. It was already past four o'clock in the afternoon, but he felt that some action had to be taken that day. He picked up the telephone on his desk and dialled an internal number. "Penelope, is Michael in?" he asked. "I would like to come and see him urgently." Michael's Personal Assistant responded brightly. "Yes, he is here. He has not got a meeting, so I am sure that he would like to see you."

Edwards thanked her; he knew that Penelope, like her boss, had been cleared to the highest level of security and was able to read all the Top Secret intelligence that passed over Michael's desk. Michael held the official position of "Custodian" within this government organisation; he was responsible for the custody, control and dissemination of all Top Secret material that was held within it. Some years before, he had personally arranged for Edwards to be specially cleared to read such Top Secret material, and would occasionally ask Edwards for his help in interpreting a particular piece of intelligence, from the financial point of view. This, Michael recognised, was where Edwards's particular expertise lay.

Edwards came out of his office, turned left and then began to descend the Grand Staircase. The building, which this organisation now occupied, had once been a leading London hotel. It had been compulsorily requisitioned by the government, at the beginning of the First World War, had briefly returned to its hotel status during the 1920's and 1930's, and had then been requisitioned again, at the beginning of the Second World War. The problem with its role as a hotel was that it was just too close to Whitehall, and therefore convenient for any expansion of major Government Departments. Whenever more space for government offices was required urgently, it had been targeted and had never become a hotel again.

Nevertheless, its Grand Ballroom still existed, and with its sprung floor, was ideal for the annual Civil Service Christmas Party, which incorporated the inevitable disco. It was this Grand Ballroom that Edward, Prince of Wales, had made famous, during the reign of his mother, Queen Victoria, by regularly dancing there with his favourite mistresses. The Grand Staircase was now in a state of some disrepair, and the government-green painted walls, did not add to the good impression of what had once been, a magnificent building.

Edwards turned into Michael's office; from behind her desk in the outer office, Penelope smiled at him. "Go on in," she said. "I have told him that you were coming." Although there were no red and green lights above the inner door, why was it that Edwards's mind always turned back to the scene in every James Bond film, where Bond visits the office of "M", to be given his next assignment? But Michael did not look like "M"; he had the same steely-grey hair but wore rimmed glasses and, rising from the chair behind his desk, greeted Edwards warmly.

Penelope brought in two mugs of coffee and then, at Michael's request, closed the inner door behind her, to ensure complete privacy. Edwards, as concisely as he could, explained to Michael how he had been introduced to Richard, what the background to this man was, and what Richard had told him. Finally, he came to Richard's offer of help to kill, or capture alive, Osama bin Laden.

Edwards had never known Michael to be fazed by anything, but, this time, a look of amazement came over his face. "Is this man really serious?" he asked.

"I believe so," answered Edwards. "His background and demeanour seemed to indicate that he was telling the truth, and his offer of help seems genuine."

"Nevertheless, we must check him out very carefully," said Michael. "It is too late in the day now, but tomorrow I will contact the "Friends" on a secure line and tell the right person your story."

Edwards knew who Michael meant: the "Friends" were the Secret Intelligence Service, funded as part of the Foreign and Commonwealth Office and generally known to the public as "MI6." This acronym always amused Edwards; "MI" presumably meant Military Intelligence, although this organisation had nothing to do with the Military. Neither did its sister organisation, known as "MI5," which was properly known as the Security Service, funded by the Home Office and responsible for domestic security and intelligence.

If people used these acronyms, Edwards always felt inclined to ask them where they thought MI1 through to MI4 had disappeared to? He, of course, knew the history of how these organisations had grown up out of the War Office, before the First World War, and that the remnants of Military Intelligence were now represented by the Defence Intelligence Staff at the Ministry of Defence. They still carried out the specific military intelligence role, assessing the real military capabilities of both friendly and unfriendly nations.

"There is not much more I can do tonight," said Michael, rising again from his chair. "I will, of course, contact you immediately I have something to report. Fortunately, I know the Head of the Middle East Section, at the "Friends," very well, and it is he that I will speak to tomorrow." The interview over, Edwards returned to his office.

Before leaving every night, Edwards's last task was to carefully lock all of his steel filing cabinets, which contained copies of all the documents that had been sent to him or that he had generated. The majority of these were officially classified as Restricted, Confidential or Secret, on a scale rising with their sensitivity. Top Secret documents, had to be returned to a central registry overnight and were kept in an even more secure environment. No government documents were ever supposed to leave the offices, except when they were carried by officials, authorised to take them for meetings with other civil servants. Edwards knew that his room, although locked overnight, could be entered by the security personnel, who held a master key. They would carefully check that he had complied strictly with their security requirements, and that he would be reported to his superiors, if he had not done so.

# 5

Nothing happened the following day about this matter except that, in the afternoon, Derek called Edwards to ask how he had left it with his contact. "You know that I cannot speak on the telephone," Edwards had told him. "We must meet up. Will six o'clock tomorrow evening be alright with you?" They had agreed to meet, at that time, at a wine bar in Chelsea, which seemed to be one of Derek's favourite places to meet. "We must find a quiet corner to talk, just you and me," Edwards had stipulated. Edwards did not want to push Michael for any answer; he knew that he would be involved in a difficult discussion with his colleagues in the Secret Intelligence Service. Patience was required, while they carried out their own checks on Richard and then carefully decide how they wanted to handle this covert approach and the offer that had been made.

At about eleven o'clock the following morning, Edwards was in his office, when, his internal telephone rang. It was Penelope. "Michael would like to see you urgently," she said. "Of course," said Edwards. "I will come straight away."

When the inevitable two mugs of coffee had been brought in by Penelope and she had left and closed the inner door behind her, Michael looked straight at Edwards.

"You have caused a firestorm!" he said. "The "Friends" listened to what I had to tell them and then they checked out this man, Richard, very carefully. But, what they found out is not good news! Did you know that he has a criminal record?"

"What?" gasped Edwards. "I was never told that. What was he charged with?"

"He received an eighteen-month prison sentence, but was released from prison for good behaviour, after only nine months," Michael replied. "He was charged with and found guilty of the possession of an illegal weapon. An automatic pistol was found in his flat. Because of this, the "Friends" are finding it very difficult to decide what to do. They have been warned by the Security Service, whom they have spoken to, that this man is unreliable and that they should not deal with him."

After that revelation, Edwards could only tell Michael that he was meeting Derek that evening, and that he would tell him about what Michael had just said. "If he knew this already," said Edwards, "he should have told me, and I would, of course, have told you."

The rest of Edwards's day was uneventful, and, in the late afternoon, Edwards took an Underground train to Chelsea and walked to the wine bar where he was to meet Derek. He was already there; he was at a corner table for two, with two glasses in front of him, and an already opened bottle of red wine. He was sipping wine from his own half-filled glass. "Evening, Colonel!" he called to Edwards brightly. Derek always called Edwards "Colonel", because the civil service rank that Edwards held, was equivalent to the rank of a full Colonel in the British Army. Edwards joined him and sat down in a rather uncomfortable wooden chair at the small table. The wine bar was filling up rapidly, and the noise level was now rising, which, to Edwards, meant that they could talk more easily, without being overheard.

"How are we this evening?" asked Derek in a friendly manner, as he poured red wine into Edwards's glass.

"Not very well," replied Edwards, "after what I was told this morning!" Derek looked at him quizzically. "Did you know that your contact has a criminal record?" asked Edwards, deciding to plunge straight into the topic that had been on his mind, for most of the day.

"Sure, I knew," responded Derek.

"Why ever did you not tell me?" demanded Edwards. "You should have known that it would influence the way that people would look at him."

"But he bought the gun for his own protection, after his wife was killed," responded Derek. "I did not think that it was important."

"I think that you had better tell me the whole story," said Edwards sternly.

Derek refilled his own glass and settled back in his chair. As always, Edwards noticed that he liked his red wine. He tended to drink it at least twice as fast as Edwards, who just took sips from his glass.

"He told me that after his wife was murdered by the Iraqis that he feared for his life," began Derek. "He asked around and someone told him to go to a particular public house in the East End of London. There, he met a man who said that he could get him a gun and some bullets to fit it. He went back there one evening, and paid for the gun in cash."

"But he had no licence for it?" asked Edwards.

"No," said Derek. "He kept it under his pillow at night. Then, early one morning, his front door was broken down and armed Police Officers stormed in. He did not even have time to reach for his gun. Maybe, that was fortunate, or they might have shot him. Instead, they searched his flat, found the gun and arrested him. He was charged with having an illegal weapon. But he said that they were from Special Branch, and he thought that they were put up to doing this search by the Iraqi Secret Service. I thought that if I told you all this, you would not have treated him seriously."

# 6

As he watched Derek at last tell him this full story, Edwards reflected on his friend's naivety. Sometimes, this man just did not seem to live in the real world! A year before, Derek had contacted Edwards and said that he had an important matter to discuss. When they had met, he had shown Edwards some documents.

"These are Gold Certificates," he had told Edwards excitedly. "I was given them by a senior Government official in Jakarta. They represent part of a hoard of gold bars, that the late President Sukarno of Indonesia, stole from the Indonesian National Treasury. The government there now want to get their money back. If you can find a buyer for them, I can share with you the large commission that I have been offered!"

Fortunately, Edwards had developed a good contact at the Bank of England and had asked his contact for help. He was told to telephone a special department at the Bank, which dealt with such things, and make an appointment. When the meeting at the Bank had been set up, Edwards had taken Derek along with him. Derek had obviously been impressed by the occasion; after they had entered the great double doors of the Bank of England, they had been received by a Bank Attendant in his traditional uniform of morning suit and shocking pink waistcoat and tie. Some of his colleagues, in the vast foyer, were wearing their top hats!

The traditions of the Bank of England went back centuries; while the great outer walls of the Bank, designed by Sir John Soane in the eighteenth century, remained, the building had been extended and improved between the two World Wars. They were led along long corridors, whose floors were covered by exquisite mosaics, and up magnificent staircases, until they arrived at a small office. There a distinguished man, in an impeccable three-piece suit, listened carefully to Derek's story. He then asked to see the Gold Certificates.

"May I take these away for a moment?" he asked politely. He returned a few minutes later, and handed the Gold Certificates back to Derek.

"I thought so," he said. "But I just wanted to check. I know the man who forged these and the exact house where these certificates have been printed. It is in the East End of London. It is all part of an international confidence trick that is well known to us. They would have led you on, with noises of encouragement, and then have asked you for a fee, plus expenses, before going any further. If you had paid this fee, you would have lost your money and never heard from them again."

Edwards well remembered Derek's astonished face at this revelation; it had taken Derek weeks to accept that, in the end, he had been a victim of attempted fraud. But there had been more amusing episodes in their relationship. Edwards remembered well a trip to Quebec he had made, with Derek, during the winter, some five years before. He could not recall why they had made this visit, but it had taken place before Edwards had joined his current organisation. He and Derek were then jointly acting as consultants to the Chairman of a leading engineering company.

They had flown first to Holland for a number of meetings. Then they had returned to Amsterdam Airport and boarded a seven-hour Royal Dutch Airlines flight to Montreal. They had been met at Montreal Airport and taken, by car, north to a small town in Upper

Quebec, where they were to have a meeting the following morning. As there were no hotels available in this small town, they had been offered the use of an empty house for the night. Their first shock had been when they got out of the car; there was at least six inches of snow on the ground. Their black city shoes were soon leaking, as they slowly made their way to the front door of the house.

It was an unusual Canadian home; there was one bedroom on the ground floor and upstairs, several bedrooms, off a square internal balcony, which overlooked the large living area. By this time, Edwards was exhausted; the early flight to Amsterdam that morning, the meetings in Holland, the long flight to Montreal and finally the drive to this small town, had taken their toll. He stumbled into the downstairs bedroom. "I will be fine here," he told Derek. He heard Derek climbing the stairs, as he was taking off his clothes. He fell into the bed, and was soundly asleep in less than two minutes.

In the middle of the night, he was awakened by a great commotion. Derek was shouting loudly that there was something moving about on the roof of the house. Fortunately, Edwards had, after finishing at university, spent some time in Canada, and even in his tired state, realised what was happening.

"Don't worry," he shouted back. "It's only a bear on the roof. It's warm up there, with our central heating on, and it's a great place for it to sleep." He then wished that he had not said this.

"A bear!" screamed Derek. "A bear! It could get in!"

"Don't worry!" shouted back Edwards, to the terrified Derek. "It's probably only a small brown bear and it can't get in. Go back to sleep."

Fortunately, Derek could now see the funny side of what had happened. When he wanted to remind Derek of this incident,

Edwards used to quote to him perhaps the most famous stage direction in any play that has ever been written. In Act III of "*A Winter's Tale*" by William Shakespeare, the unpleasant character Antigonus, has his final stage direction, before he is killed offstage. It is "Exit, pursued by a Bear!"

# 7

By now, Derek had nearly finished off the first bottle of red wine. "He must have drunk four glasses, against my two glasses," thought Edwards. "But it does not seem to have much effect on him."

"Shall we get another bottle?" asked Derek.

"Only if you want to drink more," replied Edwards. "I have had enough. It's Friday evening, and my wife will not expect me home too late."

Nevertheless, Derek ordered another bottle of the same red wine and they continued their discussion for another hour.

"I really cannot understand it," said Derek. "What does it matter that this man has a criminal record? He bought a gun, because he was scared for his life. He has a perfect excuse for what he did. You tell me that he has offered to help Britain, in some way, but you can't tell me how. How does his buying a gun in the past, affect his offer to help today?"

Edwards felt that Derek had a point in what he was saying. He stood up, now determined to leave. "Well, there is nothing further that we can do now," he replied. "It is the weekend. I will bring these points up with Michael on Monday. Now I really must get home. Have a good weekend, and I will be in touch again next week."

Edwards was true to his word; on the Monday morning, he called Penelope and asked to see Michael again. Michael was busy all morning, but Penelope made an appointment for them to meet at three o'clock in the afternoon. When he arrived at Michael's office, he was shown straight in. "Coffee?" asked the ever-helpful Penelope. "No, I have just had one, thank you," replied Edwards. Penelope shut the inner door.

"Michael, I have been thinking about this," said Edwards. "Derek has annoyed me by not telling me first about Richard's criminal record, but how does that affect his offer of help now? This seems to me such an important matter. It has such potential, that the fact he bought himself a gun, some years ago, because he feared for his life, should not affect what he has now offered to do."

Michael nodded. "I have been thinking about it myself over the weekend," he said. "It does not make much sense. The "Friends" seem to be stuck, because they asked the Security Service for their view of Richard and that is what they got back. They cannot really go against that advice. So what I have decided to do is to speak to the Security Service, at a high level, and see if I can persuade them to change their mind. They can then change their advice to the "Friends.""

Edwards thanked Michael for seeing him and then returned to his own office. The rest of the working day seemed to speed by; he was soon home eating his dinner. But the problem he had, still kept coming back into his mind. How could the offer that Richard had made, perhaps at the risk of his own life, to help the West to deal with such a dangerous man, just be ignored? He would have to rely on Michael to sort the situation out; he knew that he had contacts at the highest level in both the "Friends" and the Security Service.

But, was there a motivation here that he just did not understand? He knew that the world of intelligence was "a world of shadows and mirrors." What might lie behind the advice, that one intelligence agency gave to another? He found that he could not deal with all these questions, and decided instead to sit in front of his television set and watch his favourite comedy show.

The following day at the office was uneventful; it consisted of reading a selection of leading newspapers, which he always did to keep up with the world news. There were a few telephone calls to be answered, and then he answered some memos that had been sent to him. He still liked to dictate these answers to be typed by his Personal Assistant, who worked for him and one other senior civil servant. At lunchtime, he ate at his desk, the sandwiches that his wife had made for him at home that morning. In the afternoon, he wandered around the building. He went to see some of his colleagues, if they were free, he sat down in their offices and talked through a few problems that they might have with specific projects that they were working on.

On returning to his office, he found an urgent written "PQ" to be answered had arrived. Parliamentary Questions or "PQs" are placed by Members of Parliament, from both sides of the House of Commons, to be answered by Ministers. They can either be in a written form or, sometimes, if important enough, can be verbally asked in the Chamber of the House of Commons itself. It amused Edwards that the public thought that Ministers, even Prime Ministers, answered these questions themselves from their own knowledge. Instead, civil servants, such as himself, were always charged with answering them.

The outside public's view of government was that the elected politicians controlled everything. Instead, Edwards, like all within government, knew that the politicians, in reality, had very little real power over everyday affairs. They were temporary amateurs within a system that was run by permanent professionals. It was the civil servants who answered "PQs", answered letters from the public, drafted the politician's speeches and advised them as to their options, including on matters of policy, to help try and solve the problems that faced them and the country. As he answered this "PQ" Edwards could not but remember the B.B.C.'s very successful comedy series "Yes, Minister", which so accurately reflected the true position within government.

When asked by outsiders, to try and explain what went on inside government, Edwards used to compare his experience inside government with his experience working within major commercial companies in the private sector. "Business is management from the top down," he used to say. "The Chairman, Chief Executive and the Directors decide what direction the company will take. Within government, it is management from the bottom up. Even quite junior civil servants, can decide what is to be done. If their decision is then supported by their seniors, then it is a very foolish Minister, who will try and overturn it."

# 8

The same seemed to apply to the intelligence services. While they were sometimes "tasked" by Ministers, under advice from their senior civil servants, to carry out certain actions or investigations, most of the time they "ran their own show", in a logical and professional manner. They had their own priorities, practices and beliefs, as did other, more overt, Government Departments. It was this inbred situation that, Edwards knew, Michael was facing, as he tried to change the mind of the Security Service. If he could persuade them to change their advice, then maybe the Secret Intelligence Service would look seriously at Richard's offer.

He knew that, as between overt Government Departments, there were often serious "turf wars" between the various parts of the intelligence community. There were always arguments between them, and during the "Cold War", between the West and the Soviet Union, the fact that certain members of these secretive organisations were found to be spying for the other side, led to terrible recriminations and suspicions between the competing parts of the intelligence "machine" and between the various countries of the "Western" alliance.

The following day, at about three o'clock in the afternoon, he received an internal telephone call. "Can you come and see Michael now, please?" asked Penelope. He made his way to Michael's office, wondering just what to expect? After the mugs of coffee had been delivered by Penelope, and the inner door was firmly shut, Michael turned to him.

"I am very sorry," he said. "I cannot believe it myself, but the Security Service is refusing to change their view on this man, Richard. The fact that he purchased an illegal gun and went to prison for his crime, seems to be fixed in their mind. They believe him to be unreliable and dishonest and so cannot recommend to the "Friends" that they should even meet him."

Edwards was shocked; he thought that Michael was rather shocked too by this stubborn intransigence. "Is there nothing more that we can do?" Edwards asked.

"I am afraid not. I have tried everything that I can think of," replied Michael.

"What can I tell Derek to pass on to his man Richard?" asked Edwards, somewhat desperately.

"All you can do is be honest," replied Michael. "Just tell him that there is no interest in taking up Richard's offer of help and leave it at that."

So that is what Edwards had to do; that afternoon, he telephoned Derek and asked to meet him for lunch the following day. He thought that the least he could do was to return his hospitality and blunt the bad news, in some way, by buying him a decent lunch. "Be at my Club at 1 o'clock," he said.

Edwards was now a member of a London Club, not far from his offices. It occupied an impressive, purpose-built corner building, dating back to the 1870's and had a large sitting room, a cosy bar and an ornate dining room, with a daily selection of plain but wholesome food. More importantly, for Derek, he thought, it had an excellent cellar of good wines. Before the lunch, he would have to think through very carefully, how he would convey this decision to Derek. Furthermore, he knew that Derek would ask him what he, Derek, should now say to Richard? What explanation could he give Richard for this seemingly stupid decision?

At a quarter to one the next day, Edwards left his office, on the short walk to his Club. He wanted to be there in good time. Needless to say, Derek was late; he always seemed to be late whenever Edwards invited him anywhere! He arrived at twenty minutes past one; "We had better go straight up to our table," Edwards told him. "I booked it yesterday for 1 o'clock, and they don't like you being late." They ascended the Club's magnificent staircase with the portraits of leading past Members of the Club on either side. The Head Waiter showed them straight to their table. "Do you want a drink before lunch?" asked Edwards.

"No, just a bottle of their good Claret," replied Derek. "Oh, and I suppose we'd better have some water as well, but they do say, that water rusts your insides!"

Their meal was selected quickly; they had similar tastes. "Devilled Whitebait for two and then two Club Grills," Edwards told the waiter.

Derek grinned. "And after that, Welsh Rarebit," he said.

It was not until they had started to eat their very large Club Grills, that Edwards approached the difficult news that he had to give to Derek.

"I have some bad news for you," Edwards told Derek. "I am sorry to say that, even Michael, has been unable to change the minds of the people he has been talking to."

Derek looked somewhat shocked. "But why is this?" he asked. "I still cannot see how something that happened several years ago, can affect what my man is offering to do for us today. Why are they even refusing to reconsider this and agree to meet him, at least, to discuss it?"

"I don't know," replied Edwards. "They really seem to be fixated on his past criminal record, and are not considering, what your man could perhaps do to help Britain now."

Derek was clearly annoyed; as he drank more of the Club Claret, and as they discussed the problem further, his frustration began to show.

"In the end," he said, "I can come to only one conclusion. Someone has got to our people. It is the Iraqis again. They arranged for the raid on my man's flat, and now they continue to blacken his name. There must be someone inside our organisation, who is working for them."

"I am sorry that there is nothing more that Michael or I can do," responded Edwards rather sadly.

"I suppose that I will have to tell my man the bad news, that they are just not interested in him!" said Derek belligerently. So the matter was put to rest, and they enjoyed the rest of their lunch.

# 9

Some two years after these events, on 7th August, 1998, over 200 people were killed in nearly simultaneous truck bomb explosions at the American Embassies in Dar es Salaam, Tanzania, and in Nairobi, Kenya. Both attacks were linked to local members of the Islamic Jihad movement, but investigators managed to track the planning and execution of these two terrorist acts, back to Al-Qaeda and Osama bin Laden and his terrorist colleagues. The 7th of August was the eighth anniversary of the arrival of American troops in Saudi Arabia, and it was believed that, Osama bin Laden himself, chose the date of these attacks. Both attacks were carefully planned and managed, with local participants purchasing properties, vehicles and the required explosives.

The Federal Bureau of Investigation also connected some of the planning to an Al-Qaeda team located in Azerbaijan, and found that over 60 satellite telephone calls had been made by Osama bin Laden himself, to his associates in that country's capital, Baku. As a result, Osama bin Laden, was identified as the true "mastermind" behind these two terrorist acts, and his name was placed on the FBI's "Ten Most Wanted Fugitives List". Finally, the man hiding in a cave in the Tora Bora Mountains of Afghanistan had been recognised as the very dangerous man that he was!

Edwards followed these events closely; he could still not understand why Richard's offer of help had been turned down. He had to conclude that, if only Richard's offer had come two years later, some action could perhaps have been taken. Of course, by then, bin Laden had stopped flying between his base in Afghanistan and the Sudan, but maybe Richard could have, somehow, lured him to a place where he could have been captured? As it was, when Richard had made his offer, it seemed that Osama bin Laden, despite the attack on the North Tower of the World Trade Centre in February, 1993, had still not been identified, by the American intelligence agencies, as a real and present danger to the United States. This had been a failure of intelligence, not to have identified him earlier, for what he was. The Secret Intelligence Service could well have consulted the Americans about Richard's offer and, when they appeared disinterested, decided to turn it down. Maybe that was the real reason, rather than Richard's criminal record, for their refusal to take any action?

But then, there were other mistakes, in the further failures to do anything about trying to foil bin Laden's future plans. The Americans had allowed the Al-Qaeda teams to enter their country, and even allowed them to train to fly there. Each intelligence agency is made up of fallible human beings, and has its own history, traditions and beliefs about itself and others. Its analysts have their own bias and assumptions. It is, therefore, most important to practise complete objectivity and always to seek confirmation or "collateral" on what information is received, or on what appears to be the position. Agencies are also under the direction of their "political masters", who may well misdirect them, away from areas of research and surveillance that should be of more immediate concern.

Just three years later, early in the morning of 11th September, 2001, Al-Qaeda's second attempt to destroy the "Twin Towers" of the World Trade Centre in New York was successful. Four carefully coordinated Al-Qaeda attacks were made, by seizing four American civil airliners, which were hijacked, in flight, by a total of 19 Al-Qaeda operatives. Two of these planes were then flown into the North and South Towers of the World Trade Centre, respectively, and within one hour and 42 minutes, of the beginning of the attack, both 110-storey towers had collapsed.

Another aeroplane was flown into the Pentagon in Washington D.C., causing the partial collapse of that building. The fourth airliner was steered towards Washington D.C., for a possible attack on the White House, but crashed in a field in Pennsylvania, after some of the passengers had bravely tried to overcome the hijackers.

These attacks killed 2,996 people in total and injured over 6,000 others. If they had taken place just a few hours later, the Twin Towers would have been full of workers and the death toll would have been many times higher than it was. It is a mystery, why the hijackers did not take later flights that day, in order to achieve maximum casualties. The attacks were estimated to have cost at least ten billion United States dollars in damage to property and infrastructure alone, and some three trillion dollars in total consequential costs, including the resulting economic costs to the New York economy.

As the "Twin Towers" collapsed, it was as if two earth tremors had hit Lower Manhattan. But then the full earthquake came; instead of treating these events as a heinous crime, as they had treated the first attack on the North Tower in 1993, the United States Government responded by launching the so-called "War on Terror". The repercussions of this "War" were to prove even more terrible than even the attack on the "Twin Towers" themselves!

Lashing out, in both anguish and hurt pride, the Americans invaded Afghanistan, in a coalition with other countries, to depose the then Taliban Government there. The Taliban, based on the former Mujahideen fighters, had taken over Afghanistan, after the Russian Army had left that country. The Taliban had harboured the Al-Qaeda fighters, within their country, as they had fought with many of them against the Russians all those years before. The American Government demanded that the Taliban hand over to them Osama bin Laden and the other senior members of Al-Qaeda. When the Taliban refused to do so, they invaded.

This new Afghan war, which saw the bulk of foreign troops continue to be deployed there until 2015, resulted in over 26,000 Afghan civilians being killed and 30,000 wounded. The military casualties of the Coalition Forces amounted to over 3,400 dead, and, even just within the participating British Forces, some 10,000 soldiers were injured.

# 10

In March, 2003 the United States, and a number of its allies, decided to invade Iraq and topple Saddam Hussein. This was despite the fact that Saddam Hussein, as a more secular leader, had never supported Al-Qaeda. The so-called Western "intelligence" that was put forward at the time, that Saddam Hussein had "weapons of mass destruction", proved completely false. None of these "weapons" was ever found. Again a failure in intelligence seems to have played its part. Too much reliance was placed on the views of one Iraqi agent, now resident in

Germany, who had reported to his intelligence "handlers" what he thought they had wanted to hear, rather than the facts.

The situation was compounded by Saddam Hussein himself, who had continued his clandestine purchases of the components and materials that were needed to make chemical and biological weapons. But Saddam Hussein appears to have stopped making these kinds of weapons, after the end of the first Gulf War in 1991. So all these illicit new purchases went to waste in an attempt to bluff his enemies. His motive seems to have been to deter an invasion of his country by the Western countries, which, he assumed, were aware of his purchases. But this charade "backfired" against him; Western intelligence had indeed detected these continuing component purchases and had then assumed a serious intent to use them to make new "weapons of mass destruction."

Unfortunately, intelligence agencies are staffed by human beings who can make mistakes, and can be led astray by their informants, without they check out what they are told very carefully. Sometimes, their findings are either ignored or perhaps inflated by their "political masters" for their own hidden agendas and motives. The latter seems to have happened with the Second Gulf War; politicians in both America and Britain went out of their way to exaggerate the dangers of Saddam Hussein and the risk of these new imagined weapons to their countries. So they went ahead and attacked Iraq.

This new Gulf War continued until 2011. It resulted in the unintended consequences of the strengthening of the Iranian position in the Middle East, the growth of the even more radical Islamic State and the destabilisation of Iraq and other large parts of the Middle East. Nearly 4,000 American soldiers were killed in Iraq, and over one million were estimated to have been wounded. Over

180 British soldiers and civilians were killed and many wounded. It is estimated that between half a million and one million Iraqi civilians were killed in this largely unjustified war. Many more were terribly injured.

This Second Gulf War is estimated to have cost the American taxpayer up to three trillion dollars. It was the first mainly "privatised war", where leading American companies, supplied a large number of the needs of the thousands of troops and civilians stationed in Iraq. Many of these needs had been supplied, up until then, by the Armed Forces themselves. This resulted in a massive transfer of business and profits, from the American taxpayer, to a relatively small number of leading American companies.

If the total costs of the military assets, ammunition, services and supplies provided by the private sector are added together, the Iraq War produced a bonanza for corporate America. Many claimed that the Second Iraq War was about the "control of Iraqi oil", but any financial effect from this factor was insignificant, when compared with these vast American corporate gains, and the personal fortunes that the shareholders in these companies made. Were these perhaps the intended consequences of the decision to invade both Afghanistan and Iraq?

The toppling of Saddam Hussein, led to calls in other Arab countries for political change, resulting in what became known as the "Arab Spring". In most of these countries, these attempted "revolutions" proved, in the end, to be an abject failure. But this movement resulted in more civilian deaths and, in some countries, such as Libya, Syria and Yemen, in a total "meltdown" of any kind of civilised society. Today, after even more recent Western interventions, the Middle East and parts of North Africa are regions of almost total instability.

It was not until 2004, that Osama bin Laden finally claimed responsibility for the attacks on the "Twin Towers" of the New York World Trade Centre and the Pentagon. It was not until May, 2011, that the United States government managed, at last, to locate Osama bin Laden, who was then living quietly in Abbottabad in Pakistan. American Special Forces then carried out a daring helicopter raid, and finally managed to kill him, the "most dangerous man in the world."

## THE END

# Acknowledgements

It is somehow difficult to compose Acknowledgements for a book like this. It is all my own work, errors and all. Of its nature, it is not fiction, but is based on my personal experiences, rather than on any factual subject. But it is based on facts, since it contains what actually happened to me. But there are many other participants in my stories and I should, therefore, gratefully acknowledge their major contribution.

Some of these are former work colleagues and remain my friends. Others are people that I have met along life's way and they are friends also. I thank them for allowing me to write about them, although I have always changed their names, in an effort to protect their identities.

Some of them have read these stories, in a rawer form, before they were properly proof-read and made, perhaps, more readable. Some have also read some of my Shorter True Stories which, if this volume goes well, could become a second volume of my experiences. For those friends who have expressed their interest and their encouragement, I truly thank them. Some of them have also kindly contributed their own memories, which have helped me get more details accurately down into print.

I should also like to thank my wife, who has had to put up with my long absences on the computer keyboard. My daughter has also made a computer file of my Collected Works, so that they would not be lost to posterity.

But most of all I would like to thank my readers. I hope that they will enjoy some of these, my meanderings through life, and that they will

Lightning Source UK Ltd.
Milton Keynes UK
UKHW010646291021
393032UK00001B/47

9 781802 271072

realise that we are all the products of our lifetime of experiences, however short or long that might prove to be.

Finally, I would like to thank my publishers, Publishing Push, who offer an amazing service, at an inexpensive price, to budding authors like myself. It was once said that "we all have a book within us." They have helped to make this happen and shown great patience, despite long delays, caused by me, in the progress towards publication. With publishers like these, people's deepest ambitions can be fulfilled and others can read their work and, through that work, add also to their own lifetime experiences.

In the end, that is what human civilisation, is about. It is necessary for the "torch of knowledge and life experience", to be passed from one generation to the next. Otherwise, our humanity and our society will surely falter.

— London. July, 202